Business NOT as Usual

"Dr. Diyari Abdah has done an astounding job! This book takes you on an empowering journey. Diyari has created a must-read in the small-medium business category! A powerhouse of practical and workable plans and a road map to success. Anyone planning for a successful business recovery needs to read this book and keep it in their reference library."

—**Jack Canfield,** *New York Times* bestselling author, co-author of *The Success Principles: How to Get from Where You Are to Where You Want to Be*

BUSINESS
NOT
AS USUAL

*Success Strategies for building
a Pandemic Proof business*

DR. DIYARI ABDAH MBA MSc

NEW YORK

LONDON • NASHVILLE • MELBOURNE • VANCOUVER

Business NOT as Usual

Success Strategies for Building a Pandemic Proof Business

Published in New York, New York, by Morgan James Publishing. Morgan James is a trademark of Morgan James, LLC. www.MorganJamesPublishing.com

ISBN 9781631953422 paperback
ISBN 9781631953460 Case Laminate
ISBN 9781631953439 eBook
Library of Congress Control Number: 2020946896

Cover Design by:
Creative-Artz

Interior Design by:
Christopher Kirk
www.GFSstudio.com

Morgan James is a proud partner of Habitat for Humanity Peninsula and Greater Williamsburg. Partners in building since 2006.

Get involved today! Visit
MorganJamesPublishing.com/giving-back

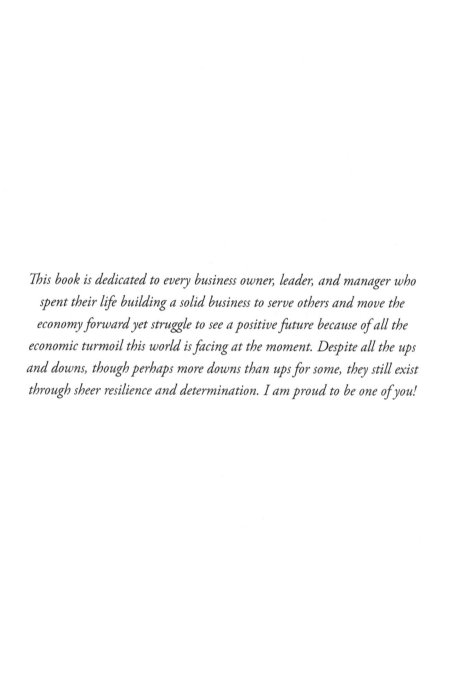

This book is dedicated to every business owner, leader, and manager who spent their life building a solid business to serve others and move the economy forward yet struggle to see a positive future because of all the economic turmoil this world is facing at the moment. Despite all the ups and downs, though perhaps more downs than ups for some, they still exist through sheer resilience and determination. I am proud to be one of you!

CONTENTS

ACKNOWLEDGMENTS

To the amazing people and friends, I have met in my life who shared their wisdom with me, gave me advice, were my mentors and extended a helping hand when needed. I will never forget you.

To my dear friend and brother, Tom Ziglar, for his tireless efforts to help others, for making today better than yesterday, for the value he adds to my life and for a great friendship that I cherish.

And, of course, to my parents, who have always been there for me and love me for who I am; to my two sons Dilan and Alan, who always make me proud and are the reason I do what I do in life; and, of course, to my wife for her dedication and continuous support over the past thirty years.

Finally, many thanks to my publisher, Morgan James Publishing, for seeing the vision of my message and supporting *Business NOT as Usual.*

FOREWORD

What if? What if "business NOT as usual" is a good thing?

I can assure you this book, written by my good friend, Dr. Diyari Abdah, is a good thing.

Is business NOT as usual a good thing for you? I have good news for you: It is if you decide it is!

The COVID-19 pandemic has turned the business world upside down. Entrepreneurs and business owners are facing challenges they had never dreamed of. And yet, these challenges are simply opportunities in disguise. I like to keep things simple, just like this book does: Successful businesses solve problems, and they are run by business owners who understand this. Can you recall a more problem-filled business climate in your lifetime? I can't! Opportunities are everywhere!

What I love about this book is that it identifies the problems every business owner is facing and then focuses on the solutions for each of them. This is a key concept: Identify the problem, then focus on the solution. Focusing on the problem is a recipe for disaster.

As you look at you and your business, what problems/OPPORTUNITIES have you identified in the following areas:

Your mindset and beliefs about the current business climate?

The attitude, mindset and skills of your people?

The new challenges your customers and clients are facing?

Business NOT As Usual is the edge you need to seize the enormous opportunity facing you and your business. Throughout history, the greatest trials are followed by the most incredible transformations and innovations by those who understand that while they cannot change the circumstances, they can change the way they see the circumstances, and then take action to develop themselves and their team members so that they can serve and solve the problems of their customers. If this sounds like you, or the business owner you want to become, then jump right in and get started devouring this book!

—Tom Ziglar, CEO of Zig Ziglar Inc.

INTRODUCTION

I never planned or foresaw writing a book like this, or any book about this topic for that matter. No one could have ever anticipated that, one day, we would live in a time of isolation and fear. Fear of shaking hands with each other, or sitting next to a fellow passenger on a plane and having a friendly talk, and, worse, fear of touching and hugging a loved one.

Many of our habits have changed forever, and new 'norms' are in place of old habits.

All the rulebooks have been torn up, and new chapters have been written; new rules will apply from now on.

In wartime, despite the devastation and damage, you know where you stand. You know who and where the enemy is, and what it takes to conquer them if you have the will and the power. When the war is over, life, in a way, slowly goes back to some normality, despite everything. Enemies forgive each other; some become even good friends and allies.

This is because we are human, and we are resilient, and we learn from history. History leaves clues and patterns, which have been studied thoroughly and deeply by many.

A virus, on the other hand, is a different kind of enemy all together. There are no peace treaties, no trade agreements or coalitions.

Standing in the face of natural disasters is another example of human resilience. The world is full of earthquakes, fires, floods, tsunamis, storms, avalanches, typhoons and volcanos. Working with nature, despite its sometimes "unkind" actions, humans have managed to stand up again and rebuild what was damaged.

Once again, this is because humans have a long history with nature, the good, the bad and the ugly, and lessons have been learned from disasters and the unforgiving turn of nature. We stand up again and rebuild our world once more.

Again, life goes on, sometimes even better than before, except for the losses we endured, the human sacrifice and loss.

Historically, after all nature has thrown at us, businesses, both small, medium and large, have stood up on their feet again, ready to move the economy around. We were back, shaking hands and hugging loved ones, eating together, enjoying a cup of coffee two feet away from a fellow human being in a café, or sitting for countless hours on a flight next to a stranger.

That used to be our 'normal' despite everything that had happened before.

Now, the world has changed, and it is not an exaggeration if we say that it has probably changed for many years to come. Perhaps an entire generation may never see or relive the 'old ways' of doing things.

As a mature human being, I feel that I am finally entitled to use the phrase "back in my day," if not for any reason but to annoy my future grandchildren, who will probably see a different world altogether. I just hope that the list of "back in the day" scenarios is not an epically long list of things we used to do and now cannot because the world has changed.

Despite the slightly gloomy start, this book is about hope, and human resilience, and what we can achieve once we put our minds to it.

But, for that to happen, we need to understand the nature of the problem, and face the new reality that business is no longer 'as usual.'

Adapting and aligning ourselves to the new reality can only help us stand taller in the face of new challenges.

On the personal level, the challenges are huge, and I am sure this will be the topic of many hundreds, if not thousands, of books and publications.

As an avid student of life, I feel it is my responsibility to be part of the solution by presenting the result of my constant research into the history and lives of others, especially business owners, who fascinate the world with their resilience and the way they deal with devastating situations. There will be very few names mentioned in the book, as the aim is to look at human resilience in general.

Everyone has been affected one way or another by the current global pandemic, and business owners (small, medium and large) have been affected, both personally and economically; therefore, this book is particularly aimed at the small and medium-sized business owners, some of whom lost literally everything in a very short time. In most business markets, we hear stories of one or two out of every five businesses going under, which is shocking.

Not to downplay other natural disasters the world has seen in the past, or the way they wiped out some businesses completely, but the global nature of the current pandemic makes getting back to business as usual an even a greater challenge, as entire supply chain systems have been affected.

Imagine a small business, like your favourite corner café and restaurant establishments, or even a doctor or dental office. These businesses are among many who have been badly affected by social distancing rules, as they depend on face-to-face interaction, sometimes at a very close proximity.

During the pandemic, I couldn't help but think about certain establishments I knew, especially those in London, and how they may survive in the future.

My love for musical instruments often took me to the Yamaha Music store in London. Near this store, just a few weeks before the pandemic, I enjoyed an amazing cup of coffee in a very small café where only four to five people could be seated at any one time.

Since the lockdown, I have been thinking about this place often, almost like a recurring nightmare, thinking what might have happened to them.

I am certain that we all have these sorts of places in mind, places that we used to go to, but, unfortunately, we may never see again.

The same goes for Tokyo, Paris, New York, Madrid, and all other cities around the world, where these small establishments and the supply chains above them kept things moving in the economy.

For that small pleasure of one cup of coffee, many people were part of the supply chain. Imagine all of that stopping—and that's just one cup of coffee!

I am not even going to touch on topic of large businesses, such as the airline industry and cruise companies. They need their own version of a *Business NOT As Usual* manual!

I realised that, though this book was thirty years in making, the tipping point was the current situation the world is facing. I have been in business for almost thirty years, and all the experience I accumulated over all those years can be found in this book.

In this book, I am trying to make some sense of what the situation is for small and medium-sized businesses, and the problems they are facing in today's challenging times, along with certain suggestions and solutions that may help these businesses in their recovery process.

These are well-thought out and well-researched solutions, by scholars, academics and, most importantly, business owners and leaders themselves.

I am not claiming that I have all the answers. No one can claim that, because we have never faced anything like this in this generation. There are no rulebooks, no manuals and certainly no one can claim to be an expert in solving today's problems based on prior experience.

Even governments are scrambling and winging it, trying to figure out what happened, doing their best or maybe their worst to reassure the public. The fragility of their knowledge is alarming; it's putting many thousands of lives at risk.

We also have to bear in mind that we cannot predict the future; any attempt or suggestion regarding future success is made based on what we know so far. Therefore, any information in this book should complement what you already know, so feel free to add them to your version of the solutions. This is merely an attempt to remind ourselves about our capabilities and certain paths we can take to once again become and stay successful. We can do it!

It's very important that any ideas from this book are done based on the reader's own judgement and information at hand; the author or anyone else mentioned in the book cannot be held responsible for the reader's actions.

I know for fact that most people who operate a business are intelligent people and can make up their own minds about what is right and what is wrong. This book is a reminder of what they may already know but can't see in this information fog, showing the business leader a path to bounce back to success using useful information the business owner may already have in their possession.

The effort of writing this book comes from the desire to help others in general, particularly small-medium business owners, by giving them some clear spectacles to see through the fog of information—or, as some call it, "mist-information!"

This book is the result of countless hours of researching the past and the present to make sense of the future.

Normally, a book like this can take anywhere from months to a decade to write, but I felt a responsibility to write this book so it will be as timely as possible. It took a good part of two and a half months of almost constant research and writing, sometimes over fifteen hours a day.

This is my contribution to my fellow human beings, and my fellow business owners, during these difficult times.

I hope you find it useful, with enough nuggets, strategies and ideas to contribute to some peace of mind for you, your family and your business, and that it propels you into a successful future.

—Dr. Diyari Abdah

PART ONE

LESSONS FROM THE HISTORY OF PANDEMICS

The global crisis caused by the arrival of COVID-19 is hitting the world hard: stock markets are collapsing, unemployment is likely to become endemic and, in several countries, mortgage and credit payments are suspended. Central banks, already hit by the systemic crisis of 2008, seem to be running out of solutions, as do our governments. In short, the health crisis could have serious social and economic repercussions and important consequences on our way of life and on our conception of social organisation.

Without necessarily considering the catastrophic scenarios, it is not difficult to imagine that there will be a 'before' and 'after' the year 2020, as was the case in 1929 and 1939.

How relaxing was it to imagine that we were somehow immune to the 'plagues' of humanity's past?

Only a short while ago, consumer society, already sharply criticised by Karl Marx over 150 years ago, was universally celebrated. Today, however, we can see all the fragility and futility of this way of life. How could we have imagined just a short time ago, as we thought nothing of carelessly wandering from one country to another, that the pandemic was already on the way, on the march across all continents? The media had warned us that a crisis was upon us. Was this carelessness the result of a subconscious desire for collective ruin, a society incapable of stopping its own destruction despite the evidence of its ill-being and alienation?

THE DIFFERENCE BETWEEN AN EPIDEMIC AND A PANDEMIC

An epidemic is the appearance and spread of an infectious disease that strikes, at the same time and in the same place, a large number of people, animals (epizootic) or plants. If the epidemic spreads over a large geographic area, we call it a pandemic (pan = all). History has left us some traces of the infectious diseases that have terrorized societies since ancient times.

Leprosy

Leprosy is quoted in the Bible, though not as a skin condition, but rather a divine punishment. The leper was removed from the community and was considered impure.

After having wreaked havoc in the Greco-Roman world, leprosy reappeared in Europe around the year 1000, causing great terror. Lepers were isolated outside towns and villages. Lepers, who were believed to be possessed, had to signal their presence by waving small bells. Leprosy practically disappeared in the 16th century. However, outbreaks have still occurred in certain geographic areas. In 2016, the World Health Organization (WHO) identified 216,108 cases worldwide.

The Plague of Athens (430–426 BC)

The first documented pandemic in history, the plague of Athens, was probably due to a typhoid fever. Described by the historian Thucydides, who was himself affected by the disease, the disease manifested itself in intense fevers, diarrhoea, redness and convulsions. Coming from Ethiopia, it struck Egypt and Libya, then arrived in Athens during the siege of the city of Sparta during the Peloponnesian War. It is estimated that a third of the city, or 200,000 inhabitants, perished during this epidemic, which also marked the beginning of the decline of Athens.

The Antonine Plague (165–190)

This pandemic was not due to the plague, but to smallpox. It took its name from the Antonine dynasty, a dynasty of seven Roman Emperors from 96 to 192 AD. The pandemic began in Mesopotamia at end of 165 during a war against the Parthians, reaching Rome in less than a year. It is estimated that it caused 10 million deaths between 166 and 189, considerably weakening the Roman population. Smallpox, caused by a virus and characterized by reddish crusts, diarrhea, and vomiting, was declared eradicated in 1980.

The Black Death (1346–1353)

After having raged in China, the bubonic plague pandemic arrived in Central Asia in 1346, spreading among the Mongol troops besieging the port of Caffa (present-day Feodosia in Crimea) on the Black Sea, which was held by Genoese merchants. The disease, manifested by horrible buboes, then spread to North Africa, then to Italy and France, where it arrived at the port of Marseille via Genoese ships.

In the Middle Ages, the plague did considerable damage in Europe. The Black Death of 1347–1353 killed around seven million people in France (out of the entire French population of seventeen million). It has been reported that the Black Death killed fifty million people in the 14th Century, which was over 50 percent of Europe's population at the time.

Diphtheria

Diphtheria has been known since ancient times. *Corynebacterium diphtheriae*, or Klebs-Löffler bacillus, is capable of producing a toxin that first affects the upper respiratory tract, then the heart and peripheral nervous system. Its epidemic evolution was stopped by vaccination in 1924. However, the disintegration of the Soviet system and its subsequent lack of mass immunization, made the disease reappear around the 1980s. In 1994, an epidemic outbreak killed thousands in Russia and Ukraine.

Cholera

Cholera is an acute diarrhoeal infection caused by the ingestion of food or water contaminated with the bacillus *Vibrio cholerae*. According to the WHO, cholera remains a threat to global public health, mainly affecting the poor living in substandard conditions.

Endemic for several centuries in the Ganges delta of India, cholera spread to Russia in 1930, then Poland and Berlin. Manifested by violent diarrhoea and vomiting, cholera causes rapid dehydration, sometimes leading to death within hours. The epidemic caused nearly 100,000 deaths in less than six months in France, including 20,000 in Paris alone. It is estimated that there are 1.3 to four million cases of cholera each year, and 21,000 to 143,000 deaths from the disease worldwide.

Flu

One the most recurring infectious diseases in modern times is the flu. The flu is a frequent and contagious infectious disease caused by four types of virus: A, B, C and D. The seasonal flu (or influenza) is composed of two viruses of strain A (generally H1N1 and A/H3N2) and a virus of strain B. It results in a set of symptoms, including fever, cough and pharyngitis. Most of the time, the flu disappears after a few days, but it can progress to several complications, such as pneumonia or dehydration, which can lead to the death of more fragile patients.

The Spanish Flu

It was also known as the 1918 flu pandemic and raged in Europe between 1918 and 1920. It was a particularly virulent strain (H1N1) that was unusually deadly. In a fifteen-month period, it infected 500 million people and killed around forty million people; some estimate this number to be even closer to 100 million deaths. It was one of the most devastating and deadliest pandemics in human history.

Like in most pandemics, there was plenty of politics involved. During World War I, to maintain morale, there were limited reports that the pandemic affected Germany, UK, France, the reports concentrated on neutral Spain, creating a false picture of Spain as being the epicentre of the pandemic, hence the name 'Spanish Flu.'

Th Spanish flu was the first pandemic of its scale caused by the H1N1 Influenza A virus; the second was the 2009 swine flu pandemic.

The Asian Flu (1957–1958)

An influenza pandemic linked to the H2N2 influenza virus, the 1957 flu was the second-deadliest influenza pandemic, after that of 1918. It caused two to three million deaths worldwide, twenty times more than the seasonal flu. Originating in China, the virus spread to Hong Kong, Singapore and Borneo. It then spread to Australia and North America before hitting Europe and Africa. A few years later, it transferred to H3N2, causing a new pandemic in 1968–1969, which was nicknamed 'the Hong Kong flu.' The latter marked the beginning of the first effective influenza vaccines. By 1957, there was a global network of biomedical laboratories linked to the World Influenza Research Centre in London, which helped in the research of the virus.

AIDS

AIDS appeared in 1981. Acquired Immunodeficiency Syndrome is the result of the destruction of immune system cells by HIV, or the Human Immunodeficiency Virus. Transmitted by bodily fluids, AIDS is a pandemic that has caused the deaths of approximately thirty-two million people, mainly in Asia and Africa.

Originally from Kinshasa in the Democratic Republic of the Congo, the AIDS virus was discovered in America in 1981, when an epidemiological agency in Atlanta, Georgia was alerted to unusual cases of pneumocystosis, which is a rare pneumonia present in immuno-compromised patients.

HIV was not identified until two years later, in 1983, by a team of researchers from the Pasteur Institute led by Luc Montagnier. At the height of the epidemic in the 2000s, two million people died of the virus each year. 36.9 million patients are living with HIV today, but antiretroviral therapy has significantly reduced mortality.

There have been other epidemics: Barcelona in 1590, Milan in 1630, London in 1665, Marseille in 1720 and the 'plague of rag-pickers' in Paris in 1920. In modern times, Egypt, Vietnam, India and Madagascar are still victims of the bubonic plague. Diseases that have struck other species have also been called 'plagues,' like bird flu or swine fever

In recent times, other epidemics have also been also documented widely, such as the Ebola virus epidemic in Africa, hepatitis C and SARS, a severe acute respiratory syndrome caused by the SARS-CoV virus, which is in the coronavirus family.

THE CYCLE OF PANDEMICS IN HISTORY

A fter the Spanish flu a century ago, and after other health crises over the decades, the economy pretty quickly recovered from the various shocks, and the economic losses were quickly compensated.

TAKING ADVANTAGE

The Zurich company Henry Michel & Co. had a sense of timeliness. On August 13, 1918, they praised their Condor electric vacuum cleaner in the newspapers under the headline:

'Spanish Flu! To eliminate all bacilli.' They also made it known that the company was looking for sales representatives.

This example illustrates how a company can adapt to extraordinary situations by reacting to possible dangers, not in the form of withdrawal, but by seeing opportunities. History is full of examples of businesses thriving on fear or devastation.

Generally, many companies react flexibly to a threat as serious as an epidemic. Above all, we usually observe a catch-up effect, which compensates for the losses suffered. However, in certain industries, such as tourism, losses are, in principle, irrecoverable.

Even during a heavy pandemic, like that of the Spanish flu, which killed between fifty and one hundred million worldwide, some companies proved inventive, as shown in the example of the vacuum cleaner company.

According to a study by Fisher Investments, the Spanish flu showed, in an exemplary way, that epidemics do not necessarily lead to a recession: In the years 1918–1919, the Dow Jones Industrial Average even climbed by more than 10 percent. "If the markets are in control of such a catastrophe, it is plausible that they will resist the current crisis," Fisher Investments concluded.

At the start of this century, stock prices behaved similarly during the SARS pandemic. The index of large companies, the S&P 500, experienced a decline of 14.2 percent between November 2002 and March 2003, but it benefited from a catch-up of 28.7 percent the following year.

During SARS epidemic, the estimated growth of the global economy was 1.0 to 1.4 percent, largely due to restrictions on international air transportation. More than 8,000 people fell ill in thirty-seven countries, but "only" 774 of them died.

ABILITY TO FORGET

Human forgetfulness illustrates how short the economic impact of pandemics can be.

In the years 1957–1958, bird flu caused more than a million deaths, including 116,000 in the United States. The stock market was running out of steam already in February 1957, when in Egyptian President Gamal Abdel Nasser ejected British and French colonists at the end of the Suez crisis.

The weakening lasted all summer, but markets recovered in the autumn, even though the pandemic was not yet under control. The same scenario occurred a decade later, when prices collapsed due to the Hong Kong flu of 1968–1969 and did not resume until mid-1970.

By the end of 1968, the virus had reached countries like Vietnam and Singapore, and, over the next few months, spread to India and Europe. American troops at war in Southeast Asia imported it to California; nearly 34,000 American victims were eventually counted.

Sometimes, the measures taken by the authorities seem to have more serious consequences than the disease itself, which is a bit like the side effects that a drug prescribed by a doctor has on a patient. This was shown in a study published by economists Beatrice Weder di Mauro and Richard Baldwin of the Centre for Economic Policy Research. Referring to 1970, they claimed that 'the measures taken by governments cause greater damage than the virus itself.'

There could be some similarity between this study and recent responses by governments around the world to COVID-19.

POORLY TARGETED, OR "TOO LITTLE, TOO LATE" INVESTMENTS

In addition to the flu, the oil price shock of the time added to the pressure on Western governments to act: 'This has resulted in inappropriate macroeconomic measures, such as stimulating inflation.' We have also seen poorly targeted and much too late investments.

All these tragic episodes have one thing in common: With a decline over a few decades, the changes are noticeable, but for the people affected at the time, they were not. Instinctively, those that are impacted always refer to the butterfly effect, where the simple flapping of wings is likely to trigger a disaster.

It is therefore natural that the number of new cases of COVID-19 were wrongly estimated on the basis of identified cases. This potentially led to bad decisions that made the situation worse, concluded a study by the Centre for Economic Policy Research.

Referring to the past, economists have shown that, usually, authorities first underestimate the effect of an epidemic and then overestimate it, or vice versa. A typical example is the swine flu of 2009–2010, also known as H1N1.

In the spring of 2009, WHO warned of a pandemic. It soon reduced its scope, but the damage was done. The result was a tsunami of vaccinations; with thirteen million doses of vaccine, worth eighty-six million dollars, the population was supposed to be vaccinated twice, though a single dose would have been enough.

In addition, swine flu did not spread as expected, and the success of the vaccination campaign was much poorer than expected. The surplus doses were offered to other countries or destroyed.

It was a poor judgement followed by a poor investment.

IMITATION EFFECTS

The fear that was felt at the time of the swine flu was due to the memory of the Spanish flu, which had a similar pathogen.

Of course, H1N1 proved to be a good deal for pharmaceutical companies, which benefited from millions of taxpayer dollars.

Authorities were not alone in misjudging the situation, as studies showed that 'consumers and businesses have delayed purchasing decisions and investments.' Such a phenomenon could prove fatal for the economy, especially when the media evokes such developments and triggers imitation effects.

From this point of view, the seller of vacuum cleaners from over a hundred years ago reacted better to the situation, even if he wrongly thought that the Spanish flu was caused by bacilli.

THE Z-FACTOR: THE MODEL THAT FORESEES THE COLLAPSE OF CERTAIN COMPANIES

In the event of a crisis, the companies most threatened are obviously those that were already in trouble.

This is measured using the Z-factor, or 'the Z-score formula for predicting bankruptcy,' which was developed in 1968 by the American finance professor Edward Altman as a model for predicting the collapse of certain companies. The model predicts that, within the SPI index, around thirty companies are particularly threatened by COVID-19.

For example:

Leclanché. Founded in 1909 in Yverdon-les-Bains, Switzerland, it produces energy storage tools, or batteries. In 2018, the company posted fifty-one million dollars in losses and still had twenty million of equity capital. The majority of the company is in the hands of a Chinese group. Lately, the Leclanché title has lost half of its value.

MCH Group. This company specialises in organizing fairs. This year, it had to cancel the Baselworld Watch and Jewlery Show and Art Basel. Given the nature of its business, MCH is obviously very affected by the coronavirus pandemic.

Meyer Burger. The solar company was once one of the stars of the stock market. However, its technology has been widely copied by the Chinese, who sell it for immensely cheaper. Since 2012, Meyer Burger has never made a profit. In 2018, its losses amounted to sixty-two million US dollars, and the share price has fallen by two thirds in the last twelve months.

Basilea. At the end of 2019, this cancer research company had 161 million in cash. Since 2013, it has continued to report losses, the latest of which amounted to twenty-two million. However, it has a strong partner: Roche. Over the past twelve months, the stock has lost 17 percent of its value and its market value has risen to half a billion dollars.

Countless books could be dedicated to the winners and losers of pandemics, and despite this book being dedicated to small and medium-sized businesses, we can clearly see that the effect of a pandemic can alter the shape of large companies as well. It is all about adaptability, resilience and the type of market.

VIRTUALLY NO TRACES

In 1919, the number of references to Spanish influenza in the Fed's monthly bulletins dropped sharply, as if the threat had disappeared. Restrictions on businesses to fight the epidemic had been lifted in most cases.

More recently, the 2003 SARS epidemic cost China a growth rate of only one percentage point that year.

We are not in an economic or financial crisis yet, say some politicians. We must avoid turning it into an economic or financial crisis. Yes, it is easier said than done, but not impossible.

The stock markets went down due to the shock of uncertainty; this is a classic situation. Markets have fallen, but there is no recession yet, and we know what to do to prevent a recession from happening.

It is a matter of political will!

Companies must be helped to retain and pay their employees, arranging payment of social charges or repayment of loans, but without being penalised later.

We must prevent economic circuits from breaking and creating vicious cycles.

Lowering interest rates does nothing to support activity.

A recession is perfectly avoidable, if there is political will.

Every new government promises to cut taxes; yet, at the first occasion, such as in the current climate, they raise taxes. In the UK in particular, the government has helped some businesses to stay afloat for a short while a small loan; however, before most businesses even could cash in on these loans, they started talking about a potential raise in taxes. A small business may not be able to tolerate and sustain all this in the long term.

IS THE EXPERIENCE OF THE CRISES OF 1929 AND 2008 USEFUL TODAY?

We hope that the lessons of the past have been learned. We have learned to avoid disasters, to some degree.

In 2000, the bursting of the internet bubble created two quarters of negative growth, but unemployment increased little. Monetary and fiscal policy in the United States had helped break the dynamics of the recession. Military spending, related to the war in Iraq, and tax cuts had helped limit the economic slowdown.

The deep economic and financial crisis of 1929 had shown that fiscal policy had to be put to use. This was done in 2008, when the United States, Europe and other countries supported economic activity through their budgets.

We also learned on that occasion that budget support should not be withdrawn too quickly. After 2008, European countries wanted to rebalance their budgets too quickly; this created a second recession in 2011–2012.

WHAT DO WE THINK OF THE TWENTY-FIVE BILLION EURO INVESTMENT PLAN ANNOUNCED BY THE EUROPEAN COMMISSION TO SUPPORT SMES AND JOBS?

Of course, this is a step in the right direction, but it is very insufficient. A close calculation shows that, in the United States alone, it would take $200 billion to support demand.

If the state pays $1,000 in payroll taxes for 150 million employees, it's already $150 billion. In Europe, each country must act in addition to the European Union. They must also support Italy, the most fragile country.

CAN STATES FINANCE SUCH MEASURES, GIVEN THEIR ALREADY HIGH OBLIGATIONS?

The short answer is 'Yes,' because certain countries, such as Switzerland, Germany and France are paid when they borrow on certain maturities, thanks to negative interest rates. This gives them room to manoeuvre.

ANALYSING THE PAST

Prior to the current pandemic, studies and reports suggested that increased human interactions, constant travelling and the manipulation of viral strains in laboratories were factors the World Health Organization (WHO) claimed would increase the chances of a viral spread during a pandemic.

To understand the present, one must analyse the past. What can we learn from the 1918 epidemic? It reveals that all the elements necessary for the appearance of a global pandemic were present; an extremely contagious infection, a variable and virulent strain of the virus, mass displacement around the world following the First World War, poor hygiene and nutrition, and medical contexts leading to death from complications induced by infection.

It was after this pandemic that the WHO was created (though it was not officially created under this name until 1948) because it demonstrated that a disease emerging in China could, with the necessary conditions met, impact very remote regions of the world, such as Europe. According to WHO data, the spacing of dangerous influenza epidemics is about thirty-nine years apart.

Past reports suggested that, if a strain similar to that of 1918 appeared, with our current lifestyles of travel to and trade with the far sides of the world, a virus could spread at an outrageous speed. In addition to influenza, there are also epidemics, such as Ebola and the coronaviruses responsible for severe acute respiratory syndromes (SARS), that worried health authorities around the world.

Obviously, the hygiene, nutritional and medical context is now better in rich countries, which could limit the spread of diseases such as the Spanish flu. Hhowever, people in poor countries would once again find themselves in great danger.

According to WHO, a virus can travel around the world in just thirty-six hours; this is due to our modern lifestyle of movement and international exchange. In addition to that, the increasingly frequent handling of pathogens in laboratories increases the risk of accidents or a strain of virus getting out of hand.

WHO, even before the current pandemic, summarised in seven fundamental points the actions needed to be taken to prepare the world to fight against a large-scale pandemic. These actions are:

- ❖ The total and unfailing commitment and investment of the governments of all countries.
- ❖ The most developed countries must lead by example; each country must build more efficient health systems capable of considering and preventing the majority of the risks of contamination.
- ❖ All people must be prepared for the worst and develop effective strategies (vaccines, if available) in the event of a pandemic.
- ❖ The world of finance must prepare crisis plans to prevent such an economic meltdown.
- ❖ Create incentives to act and obtain funding to support actions.
- ❖ Strengthening of the coordination mechanisms of the various countries by the United Nations.

If these measures are not taken seriously, poor countries would be the first to suffer heavy loss of lives (fifty to eighty million, according to the report by WHO) and serious economic consequences, all of which would cause social chaos.

This was a report pre-empting what may happen in the case of a pandemic—and, interestingly, we are currently facing one!

So, were all the seven points valid? And did everything happened as predicted?

What we must remember is that the risk of a global pandemic was always on the horizon due to the ease of travelling and the way people interact, and, if adequate precautions are not taken, according to WHO, this risk will always be there.

WHO reported prior to the current pandemic that the growing risk cannot be ignored, and that all necessary measures must be taken to not only prevent the occurrence of a pandemic as much as possible, but also to prepare for the worst if it happens. Even if our countries are, on the whole, better able to respond to this type of disaster, thanks to our health institutions, the elderly and young children may find themselves in danger during a pandemic. Adults, too, can find themselves in a life-threatening emergency due to a deadly viral infection, as was the case during the Spanish flu epidemics, and the devastation witnessed in this pandemic is proof of that.

PART TWO

HOW PEOPLE BEHAVE
DURING A PANDEMIC

B usinesses and companies are run by people, for people, to benefit from their actions, services or products. The key word here is: people!

Therefore, the way people react during hardship and threats, loss and major change is important to grasp in order to be able to understand what goes through our minds and how we can help others overcome their fears and anxieties, especially as part of a work/business recovery plan. This should be prioritised above everything else as a first step into a healthy comeback.

In his book, *The Psychology of Pandemics: Preparing for the Next Global Outbreak of Infectious Disease*, Dr. Steven Taylor, a professor and clinical psychologist at the University of British Columbia, Vancouver, Canada, explained that the emotional cost of a pandemic can be very significant and, although it varies from person to person and family to family, huge.

There is usually widespread uncertainty about the odds of getting infected. Additionally, there is uncertainty and misinformation about methods of prevention and disease management. Other psychological stressors include health threats to the family and loved ones, shortages of essential food, social isolation and disruption of routines, particularly, in this case, business and work routines, the uncertainty that comes with it in terms of total loss of revenue and income and the uncertainty of a potential recovery phase.

That is why being able to see through the information and misinformation, or 'fog,' can give some clarity and allow for some peace of mind, letting you think and rethink strategies, hence the 'Business NOT As Usual' motto. These are new times that require new thinking, along with new goals and plans.

The effects a pandemic can have on the broader economy is huge, as has been witnessed, and there is perhaps still more to come. In 2016, the National Academy of Medicine estimated that during the next pandemic (meaning this one!), the global economic cost will exceed $6 trillion; recent reports suggest figures far above that.

The majority of business owners have been affected one way or another by this pandemic, and, as mentioned before, the first item on the recovery agenda should be the people involved in the business, both employees and customers. People have been through a lot, mentally, emotionally and financially (some worse than others); to manage all that is not an easy task, but once we understand the different human emotions, we may be able to help ourselves and others in a better way. An understanding for what goes through our minds as business leaders, and the minds of our team members, can help make the recovery journey a little smoother.

Each person around us (including ourselves) has a personality, which is a collection of traits defining a person's way of thinking, feeling and behaving in situations. In addition, a person may have fluctuating degrees of a given trait. Personality traits have been linked to how ready a person is to experience a negative emotion as a response to a particular stressful situation.

According to Prof. Taylor, research has shown that people with an unrealistic optimism personality who have low-level health (pandemic) anxiety, through their non-adherence to hygiene and health recommendations, are more likely to spread contagion during a pandemic. This is important to observe among staff and team members so that the right preventative measures are taken.

In contrast, people with other personality traits, including high-level anxiety, threat overestimation and high uncertainty intolerance, are likely to become very distressed during a pandemic, resulting in health anxiety. These people will make themselves physically sick, even if they are not. They start to feel unwell, achy and sick to their stomach. They don't sleep well and feel tired all the time, and they think they have what might be going on at the time, such as a COVID-19 viral infection.

We all have witnessed colleagues, family members and others who have said they may have the infection because of a cough, sweating or just tiredness.

This can be a state or a trait, and people with excessive health anxiety can become very anxious and negative during a pandemic threat, becoming very aware of and vigilant to bodily sensations. This leads to excessive safety behaviour through seeking repeated medical reassurances, adding unnecessary burden on the business and the healthcare system.

These personality types may benefit from cognitive-behavioural therapy, according to clinicians and researchers. Exhibiting high intolerance levels to uncertainty can be associated with mood and anxiety disorders, obsessive-compulsive disorders and other clinical conditions. People suffering from this have the tendency to worry too much about many issues in relation to the uncertainties surrounding a pandemic, not just the health implications of a pandemic. The list of uncertainties associated with a pandemic can be very long, starting with the obvious, immediate health issues and risks, from the possibility of getting infected or spreading it, to the long-term effects over a period of time.

Understandably, these are sources of distress that can affect anyone, but people need to be able to accept and tolerate a level of certain uncertainty. Anyone who denies this uncertainty in their mind may become highly anxious about getting the infection.

Some people may have a 'monitoring cognitive style,' while others may have a 'blunting' style, both of which refer to the way they seek or avoid information and advice. Monitoring involves collecting and scanning for health threat information, whereas blunting involves minimising the threatening news or information. These strategies to cope with a health threat have flaws: Blunters can show little interest in health advice and may not act on it swiftly, thus risking their lives and that of others. Monitors, on the other hand, tend to amplify any health risk issue and are more vulnerable to daily stress, especially in the presence of a major health risk, such as a pandemic. Stress management training may prove helpful in these situations, but some monitors may benefit from professional intervention and psychological treatment.

These are important personality traits to understand and bear in mind when dealing with employees and team members during the recovery stage, as people (including ourselves) have been through a lot, and not everyone takes the same health advice and organisational information and instructions in the same way. Knowing how to identify and deal with each type is not an easy task and is the job of professionals but knowing the essential basics for understanding these personality types and traits may help demystify and allow you to identify certain behaviour.

The threat of a pandemic is very serious, as everyone knows, and certain people (employees/team members) may require a more professional type of help, rather than just a positive talk. Although it is not the duty of a business leader to diagnose such cases, it is important not to dismiss the impact of such a health threat on someone's mind; not downplaying it or dismissing it is crucial.

Professionals have a 'screen and treat' approach, and they know how and when to do this, so any business leader who is in doubt should seek professional help for their employees.

A true and healthy recovery cannot happen if the business has people who are overly anxious and can't perform well. They should be helped by professionals and recover first; only then can they be at their best. It is the right thing to do, as caring about your team members and employees can help the company in the long run.

Understanding the people you work with is key to a happy and successful recovery. It is not all about new ideas, or advertising and marketing, but future human interaction. This is very important, because this generation has never seen anything that has threatened their health, impacted their loved ones and continues to impact their future on this scale before. Being kind to ourselves and others and having compassion is the first step towards recovery.

PART THREE

THE BIG FIX

RISKY CHOICES

During and after global disasters, many decisions are made, mainly by authorities and governments, based on probabilities and psychophysical factors that define the degree of risky outlooks. As individuals, not all of these decisions are in our favour. Some are done based on the little information available at the time, and others are done for political points, but they are not always in the individual's favour. Businesses, especially small and medium-sized, are run by some of these individuals, who are under a tremendous pressure to 'get it right' and soon, because their resources do not allow for mistakes and redoes.

> YOUR TOOL KIT TO A SUCCESSFUL RECOVERY
>
> "DURING TOUGH TIMES, STANDARDS NEED TO BE HIGHER THAN USUAL TO ACHIEVE SUCCESS."

Decisions under risky choices mean accepting that these decisions are made without prior knowledge of their consequences. There is also the probability of matters not going as planned, which, in itself, is very tough for any small business to face, especially during a global hardship.

A choice between keeping the status quo and risk taking as an alternative is not uncommon in these situations. The question is which one yields maximum benefit for the business in question:

Not doing anything, waiting or riding out the storm, or being a risk taker? History is full of stories of businesses taking too much of a risk and failing as a result.

Both options present advantages and disadvantages, which can be unique to each business, depending on the type of market they are in, their market share and their position regarding cash flow or access to resources and funds.

LEADING THROUGH AND AFTER THE CRISIS

Great leadership may seem straightforward when times are good and business is ticking nicely. A leader's true substance, and what they are made of, will show during tougher and darker times, as that is when a leader is put to the ultimate test in leadership and managing and helping people.

Leading a business through crisis can determine the success or failure of the business at a later stage. People can behave differently during crisis. Some become quite irresponsible and act childish (no disrespect to children, as some behave far better than some adults), although this behaviour, luckily, is an exception rather than the norm, as time of crisis can also bring out the best in people.

Employees and staff can truly raise their game and become a pivotal part of the successful comeback of the business, and it is the leader's task to encourage and create the right environment in order for this to happen.

People can change during crisis and dark times, but one hopes that, despite everything, the change is a positive one. True leadership is being transparent and honest, yet also creating hope by showing the light at the end of the tunnel through the darkness. History is full of examples of leaders who saw beyond what everyone else did.

One of the crucial tools a leader has is the use of words. Chosen wisely and timely, they can improve a situation greatly and can enhance the vision of others, who may not see well during dark times. But, before getting into these crucial points, a business leader must make the wellbeing of everyone, including himself, the number-one priority.

A business leader needs to communicate the following strategic points with the people working in their business on regular basis, and more so during times of crisis.

1. How the situation is so far: Just being honest and describing the situation to the employees/staff can make people feel at ease, because now they know what is going on in the business and know you are not leaving it to the last minute just before restarting the business. They do not feel undervalued and pushed aside. These are the same people who helped make the business successful, so they deserve to know what is going on.

2. Talk about the plan: A business leader may not have all the answers yet, but they certainly have more answers than some, and sharing a plan of action can bring clarity and vision. Even if the plan is not or cannot be executed 100 percent, it is still a plan, and as they say, 'a' plan is better than 'no' plan!

3. Having a plan is part of being a leader. Invite others to contribute to the plan, being prepared to include the good ideas and decline the bad ones, making everyone feel valued and motivated to contribute.

4. Showing interest and trust in others by asking them for their opinions and what else they need from the leader in order to

move forward. A business leader may have acquired plenty of information to make a plan or a decision, but there is always room for one or more great ideas. This is important for people to hear, as it gives them a sense of belonging and importance, especially in time of crisis, where overall morale can be low, and everyone needs to feel better about themselves. A leader who knows how and when to stay quiet and listen to others is a leader who wins the hearts and minds of their organisation. Reminding people of why they do what they do and reminding them of the good times when everything was going smoothly and successfully thanks to them, will no doubt bring people back into alignment with the vision and values of the business. During tough times, standards need to be higher than usual, as only through higher standards can a leader push everything and everyone in the right direction to bounce back and recreate success. Hold everything and everyone accountable for actions; do not only point out and praise great work, but also point out mistakes to be avoided, as they can be very costly during this period.

5. A good leader praises everyone for a great job and the way they pulled together in time of crisis and should reward their success by giving bonuses if the business rebounds successfully. Create opportunities for celebrating even the smallest steps of success. Sometimes, small gestures of kindness towards staff and their loved ones can go a long way, wining their loyalty in the long run, which is needed to sustain success and thrive.

For the above points to work and engage people fully, a business leader needs to control certain elements in their own environment and mind. This is very critical.

Controlling fear is crucial; As much as fear can sometimes be healthy for certain decision making, a leader needs to subdue their fear, as people respond better to a confident leader.

In tougher times, people's perception of a confident leader can take on a different dimension as they realise everyone is in the same boat and business is not what it used to be; however, a confident leader can always get their ideas and plans across better, and can ask more from the people they are leading, simply by showing confidence.

Charging ahead blindly and demanding the impossible is not courage, but foolishness, and people will recognise it soon enough. Being in control does not necessarily mean having the courage to make decisions but rather being in control of the situation and leading people with confidence in the right direction. It is making the right decisions despite feeling fear.

No one will blame a cautious leader, but everyone will blame a foolish leader, especially if they did not think about the wellbeing of others and put the business above everyone.

This certainly will affect morale, and thus productivity and overall and long-term success.

For people, putting their trust in a leader is a privilege, and having a goal in mind that is worthy of their efforts is the job of a good leader, who will then motivate the team to deliver their best to achieve the goal, ideally at no cost to their wellbeing. That is trust, knowing that a leader is not putting anyone's wellbeing at risk to achieve a goal, and with trust always comes respect—and what leader doesn't want a healthy dose of that?

In military terms, during combat, a platoon leader is not fearless, because everyone, at some point, will feel fear of a particular situation or outcome. It could be the fear of losing men, or the battle itself. But, a courageous commander will control their fear for the sake of others, not allowing it to become contagious. Furthermore, they sacrifice their personal interests for the sake of the goal and the mission they are tasked to do. That is why others follow: They see that degree of sacrifice and willingness to be there for others.

The military, as one of the oldest institutions, has streamlined this whole process of action in times of crisis in the most efficient way (despite the author's personal opinion that peaceful solutions and dialogue should always take precedent over any military action in the world).

Business leaders, who have never experienced tough times like now, can sometimes feel powerless and not sure what the best course of action to take is. They want to put their business back on track, or maybe even make it better than before the crisis, by having contingency plans that deal with any future surprises.

TRANSPARENCY AND LEADERSHIP

If a company suddenly breaks down in sales and earnings and, in extreme cases, gets into an existential crisis, its management team is put to the ultimate test. The motto that managers should take to heart in bad times is to never hide bad news in times of emergency.

Communicate openly: Be transparent. Your employees are smart and they'll figure out when things are not right. You can feel it quickly when a problem starts to show, like a fire spreading in a building. The problem could be the volume of work or orders is falling, or management is becoming increasingly nervous and questioning privileges that were previously taken for granted. Inform your employees early if your company is in a crisis; only then can you win them over as a partner in coping with the problems.

Be honest: Inform your employees openly about the possible effects of the crisis—if possible, without designing horror scenarios.

Nothing unsettles the staff as much as things they cannot assess: Is the fire a flash in the pan? Is it limited to the roof structure, or will it also cover other parts of the house? Does it affect my work situation? The rumour mill turns, and the fire—in the minds of the employees—gets bigger and bigger. Inform the employees about what measures are or have already been taken to take care of the problem.

Show your backbone: Stand by the decisions you made to master the crisis, even if they have negative effects for some employees. Don't hide behind false facts or pretend that the banks made your decisions. This will reduce your credibility and you will not show leadership.

Providing orientation: Show your employees clear ways in which the crisis can be overcome. Use concrete examples to describe how your company or others have already mastered crises in the past (though obviously not to this global pandemic extent) so that your employees can feel that success is feasible.

Provide support: Agree with your employees' clear goals and concrete measures on what you should do to make your contribution to mastering the crisis. Ask them to define milestones to be passed on the way out of the crisis and celebrate when that milestone is reached, no matter how small.

Leadership is a choice and a lifestyle, not your personality; most leaders, or most people who qualify as leaders, become that because it's necessary for them to step into a role to achieve a goal within an organisation. Smart leaders know how to increase their tonality or when to tone it down based on what they want to achieve.

As a leader, try to have different styles. This means you should occasionally fall back, listen to others and observe or analyse what's going on around you in order to make better decisions. Other times, you need to rise to the occasion in order to motivate your people. Different situations require different styles of leadership.

It takes a good leader to know when to fall back and observe, and when to step up and motivate.

There's a common misconception that leaders always have to make the final decisions. This is not always the case, as leaders depend on the people around them to make some wise choices for them. If, in your organisation, you have people and team members whom you trust, and you trust their judgmental and honesty and you know they've got your back, sometimes it's best to fall back and delegate the decision-making to them. That way, they own it, and they can work on it full-heartedly.

During the current crisis, ideally, one should have a team that is responsible for doing different things and different tasks with one main goal, which is to help get the business back on track. What you delegate to your team members is up to you, as only you know who in your team is capable of running a certain task and how they will do it. You can decide either to give directions, or, if you trust that team member enough, they can do it by themselves.

It's assumed that some are natural leaders, but that doesn't mean they were born leaders, as leaders are built and not born. Make sure your leadership style is flexible, but flexible doesn't mean indecisive, controlling or arrogant. What it means is that your leadership adjusts to the situation and to surrounding events with one main goal in sight, namely, for your company and your business to be successful for yourself and for your team members, and to be around for a long time so that the customers benefit from your goods and services. No one wants to be part of a losing team, and as a leader, one of your tasks is to encourage your team to win most of the time. When you are leading a winning team, it becomes a privilege to work with you and under your guidance. Under your leadership, people will be happy to do what you ask them to do, and happy to come work for you. That's what true leaders do: They inspire and encourage.

How many times have we witnessed a sport team win not necessarily because they were absolutely the best, but rather because they had the desire, passion and fire inside them not to let their coach (their leader) down, because they knew letting their coach down was far worse than losing?

Make sure, as a leader, when you talk to your team members and employees, you always tell them why you ask them to do something. People need to know the motive behind what you are asking for. It could be because you want to help others, or you want to create opportunities and take your business to the next level, or you want more recognition for your business, which subsequently means more recognition for everyone in the business. Whatever the reason is, let them know. You will get a better response this way.

Every leader has a vision. This needs to be communicated, and you must try to help them buy into your vision. If you fail to make them buy into your vision, it is most likely because all you wanted was more money and nothing else. Money is important for the business, and it's why most people are in business; however, one could look at money in a different way.

When making money for the business becomes like a tool for the families of the employees to live a decent, honest and good life, then money is good. If that money is to be reinvested in people in the company to get better results, to better serve, that's even better.

No doubt, the more financially comfortable a company is, the more opportunity is created for everyone, such as better education for the children of the employees, and better standards of living, including better healthcare for the employees and their families.

However, if money-making just becomes about greed and numbers to brag about, that's where employees will lose respect. They won't buy into your vision, and when that happens, especially in the world of small-medium business, then it's a very dangerous game; when employees realise what the leader is all about, the customers will realise that too, which cannot be good for a small, personalised business. Obviously, if you are a small business selling yachts to the rich, that is a different story all together, or if all your clients are affluent, then perhaps that doesn't matter much, but even the rich don't like to be taken for granted or taken advantage of. No one likes a greedy business owner.

So, you have to ask yourself: What's your real motive and incentive for being the leader in your business? What's in your heart that makes you wake up in the morning, go and lead, and come back home to your family with a clean conscience?

What keeps you going? We hear these phrases all the time: What makes you tick? What makes you wake up in the morning? What keeps you going? Why are you doing what are you doing?

All are legitimate questions. First and foremost, you need to be truthful to yourself before you can make others understand and buy into your vision.

During the pandemic crisis, most of us had no choice but going under lockdown, and maybe reflecting on and contemplating the past, present and future.

I'm pretty sure most of us made plans for when we go back and what we will be doing.

Yes, it is true there is economic hardship, and we will have to bounce back one way or another, trying to recover fast once the pandemic is over, but there has to be some true passion behind your decision to change things for the better, for your promise yourself that you will never be in a situation where you have to worry about your business' finances, no matter what comes next.

We all made decisions and we all being passionate about it, and there is nothing wrong with that; however, if we forget about all of that the moment we go back to work, then that could become a different story altogether, with different outcomes than what you are hoping to achieve. We need to stay focused and honour our promises to ourselves.

So, think like a true leader, observe like a leader, talk like a leader, behave like a leader and be a true example for others to admire and want to buy into your vision, because that's what true leaders do. When leaders show and speak with passion, they persuade. They don't need many words; it's in the tone of the voice, in the magnitude of the words. As we said earlier, leadership is a skill that can be learned; maybe it's time to master it and be the best leader you can be, because if you are a real, passionate, persuasive leader, your business will succeed and thrive without a doubt, as long as you keep the motivation and the passion going. No doubt, your employees will give you 100 percent and then some, but you have to be persistent at it. Passion is contagious, but it also needs recharging, as it doesn't always last very long, and people need to be reminded of where you stand and why you do what you do.

You may know the why and the how, but they might not see it that way, and that's why if you don't show them the passion, then some of the ideas you present may seem impossible, and people might think you have been too demanding or too unrealistic, or even unappreciative.

We all know stories of employees leaving a company. Sometimes, one of the best employees or a key team member on whom you depend very much leaves the company because of other reasons than just money. As a leader, watch every step, watch every word that comes out comes out of your mouth, be careful about your decision-making, have other people's interests, especially your employees and, in particular, your key employees, at heart, so that, when you ask for help in a time of need, they stand right behind you and they give you their absolute best.

By the way, no amount of money can substitute their feeling respected and appreciated. When you have been there for them, they will definitely be there for you.

This lockdown might have been a golden opportunity to show true leadership, and it still is, to an extent. Show your employees you care about them, their families and their finances. Do what you can to help; there is no doubt you will see the positive results later, which is what you need in a time of recovery and beyond.

A LEADER'S FOCUS

You may or may not have noticed, but it feels like you are being watched lately.

You are being watched by your employees, wondering what your next move will be and how it will affect them. You are being watched by your customers, especially if you are in the service industry, wondering what your next move is and when you will reopen, how you will function and how safe will it be for them. Would they come just because they need you, and would they recommend their families and friends to come to you because you are the best and the safest place? This will take up a compartment in your mind, and it may cloud your thinking and judgement, or even lead to bad decisions.

Therefore, having the ability to focus on the things that matter most is probably one of the critical elements of a recovery strategy.

Remember what got us here and know that the way your business has been conducting its affairs for the last five, ten or twenty years will probably not be the same way you will be conducting business from now on.

We all know several businesses that will never be the same again, for the worse or for the better, so this is the time to focus in order to put things in perspective and make good decisions.

A lack of focus is much like a lack of vision. A lack of vision, as we know, doesn't get you anywhere; you'll be just wandering around.

Now, more than ever, your business needs all your attention and focus.

Learn how to eliminate the non-important things from your routine, or at least file them under a non-essential folder for later; right now, you should think and look at things with a different mentality and eyes than before the crisis.

Since the economic downturn of 2008, many businesses have been playing catch-up. Now there is this crisis, so to focus on what matters is one of the keys to be on a healthy recovery path. As a result, you cannot afford not to be focused. You can focus again by following these steps:

1. Eliminate clutter from your mind and your daily routine. Focus only on the things that matter the most. You need to see certain things transparently and clearly. Clarity occurs by having the correct information and data and looking at without any clutter.

   At the moment, don't worry too much about long-term future plans; hopefully, that will be in the next phase. Instead, focus right now on the task at hand, which is how to recover fast and be successful.

   If you have clarity, it means you can think better; if you think better, you can make better decisions. Making better decisions, at this moment, is what your business needs right now.

   You do not need to make 1001 decisions at the moment; the truth is that most businesses that were affected greatly by this pandemic crisis need only a handful of decisions at first in order to bounce back quickly.

   However, a handful of good and effective decisions require focus, and focus requires a small number of problems to be solved first, rather than dealing with 100 different problems at the same time.

2. In order to focus, de-clutter and narrow down your selection of problems to solve. Do the most important things first. This means picking three of the most important issues, the ones that you have to do immediately, from your list of problems; then, once you master those three and you feel comfortable, then pull another problem. When you master one issue, only pull one from the list to deal with; otherwise, they accumulate, leading to feeling overwhelmed and procrastination.

Before you know it, instead of, in a short period of time, dealing with twenty problems at once, which could lead to bad decision making, you have dealt with only three issues to begin with, and after you mastered them and made sure that everything is running smoothly, only then do you dedicate your time, resources and energy to solving the remaining ones.

Focusing like this will ultimately prove to be the best thing that you could do for yourself and your business. At the end of the day, you can only do so much in a space of time; with limited time and energy, you can only deal with so many things at any one time, and you cannot solve twenty problems at the same time in one day without jeopardising something or making a bad decision occasionally.

There will be other problems and issues that will pop up and require attention, but not everything that pops up requires our immediate attention. Even if other issues show up, at least no, you have some 'mental' space to deal with them. Since you solved the initial problems, you just need to make sure you categorise them correctly based on their urgency and importance.

Keep in mind that clarity leads to better decisions, so the more you focus on these matters, the shorter your list will get, and the clearer you will be.

3. It is all about commitment. Once you focus on the issues that matter the most, and you know what you will focus on, you commit. Commitment is doing what you say you are doing, even after the mood in which you said it has left you.

    Commitment is the glue that binds you to your words.

    Commitment is taking action. If you just identify the issues that you need to deal with and you focus on finding the solution, that's great! But, you are only halfway there. You have to commit to doing something about it, which completes the cycle.

Identifying the problems in your business, and having good intentions of doing things about them, is a good starting point, and maybe you can sell the idea to your employees, who are hopefully behind you. However, without commitment, no action will be taken, and that can be pretty bad for the business, for your reputation and for your respect among the employees. You will be known as the person who has lots of good ideas but never implements anything, which means next time, when you need their help, they probably won't take it seriously because you never take yourself seriously. The key here is 'take yourself seriously.' Commitment to fulfilling your plans is more than just taking action; it is an 'attitude.'

At the end of this process, you will realise how much your focus paid dividends.

In the past, you may have made some very good suggestions, but never followed it up for some reason. Now is the time to change all that and challenge yourself, because your business needs you.

Imagine taking a photo, and how you focus on one element that is important (a child, a flower, your favourite pet), and how you defocus, or blur, the background. Now, imagine if you could do that with the issues that matter the most. Your mind needs to be exactly like that; even though you picked three things to concentrate on, ideally, we still need to focus on each one of them separately. All three need to be done at about the same time, but each one individually deserves our sharpest and deepest focus, so you can just forget about the other ones for the time being. Set a deadline for all three, and within the main deadline set three sub-deadlines for each task.

It is all about breaking this down into manageable, bite-sized pieces that don't make us overwhelmed.

This method, if you stick to it long enough, will slowly create a routine or a system in your business for problem solving, and you can use it time and time again. You can also teach your team to do it the same way, and before you know it, it becomes your business' problem-solving culture.

Train yourself to deal with one problem at a time and resist the temptation to solve many at once, but obviously don't waste too many resources and energy on that one problem; focus and solve it, and then implement the solution.

This can be a very important experience, which you will remember every time you are faced with multiple problem-solving situations in your business. You will always focus on the number one issue and see what brings in the fastest resolution to that problem, and then focus on the rest.

In the meantime, and while you are focusing on that one important issue, don't forget to look at the big picture, too. As a good leader, remind yourself to do this often.

Remember, leadership, and everything that goes with it, is a learnable skill. So, learn and practise this aspect of leadership every day. As a good leader, train yourself to be able to focus and solve issues, while still managing to see the bigger picture.

To have those two abilities, to be able to focus and de-focus on the matters that mean the most or the least to your business, is what good leaders are all about. They always have the big picture and vision in mind, but at the same time, they can narrow down and focus on one aspect of a problem and solve it, or delegate it to the right people.

Leaders are generally positive people; they bear in mind negative outcomes and worst-case scenarios, but usually their concentration and energy are used on what would happen and how the company will benefit if they did XYZ, and what would it take to achieve that. Usually, they don't think about negative outcomes; while they always have it in the back of their mind, they try to avoid the trap of negative thinking.

Most of us have worked alongside people who cannot help but think in a negative way; in anything they plan or do, they always think something negative will happen as a result, and they plan more on how to get out of a negative outcome than how to celebrate a potential success.

Understandably, some may call that having a contingency plan, looking for ways to get out of a negative outcome, which is fair enough! However, if that's what dominates their entire thought process every time they plan or have a goal or try to make a decision, then they will probably train their minds to always think in a negative manner.

Yes, it is true that negative outcomes do happen; however, the positive usually outweighs the negative. Otherwise, no one would ever be in business.

Therefore, when you focus on anything, start positive, with the exceptional and great results that might come out of it, and how wonderful things would be for you, for the business, employees and customers if these things happened the way you wanted.

Visualise the best-case scenarios, rather than visualising worstcase scenarios. If you train your mind to think positively and always think of best-case scenarios, you will do more, achieve more and become better at solving problems when they happen, as you approach them from a positive angle, such as looking at a problem as an opportunity for improvement rather than the end of your business.

The routine of being positive, visualising and delivering results, will no doubt affect your confidence, making it grow; with it, your self-esteem and respect for yourself will grow, too, allowing you to make better judgements and decisions. In the event that, one day, there is a problem, then that's just one thing compared to the tens of good things that you have achieved, and you will have the focus, courage and resilience to deal with it and turn it into an opportunity.

The history is full of examples of resilient people who turned dire situations into opportunities and success, or even used it to their advantage as a platform to launch other successful ideas and plans.

Remember the first day you started in business?

I doubt that you started with the notion of failing immediately in mind.

You were full of hope and courage, and decided that, whatever comes your way, you will conquer it, and turn every opportunity into a successful one to serve the business.

Now you just need to 'focus' again and remember those days, learn from yourself what you did best and what you prefer to change. If there are repeated problems that cause you headaches, maybe there is a pattern, and you can change that, too.

Stay positive, hopeful and courageous, and learn skills that you are lacking while mastering what you are good at.

These crises and what come with them, in terms of a negative economy, will not last forever.

Instead of looking at the crisis as a 'doom and gloom' situation, you can say to yourself that you will make it and do everything to survive this, turning it around to your success and advantage.

For some, it is like starting all over again, but the positive difference is that you have already established yourself. You have a name and the know-how, and you are wiser than when you first started, so think of it as a semi-start-up but with more knowledge, and go forward with the same intensity and fire in your belly as when you started all those years ago, waiting for your first customer to show up.

Focus on the solutions to the problems!

When people who know you see that you have gone from survival to success by being focused, determined and finding solutions rather than paying too much attention to the negatives, they will ultimately respect you even more than before, because it will demonstrate that you are an implementer.

This way, you can also positively impact the people around you in a way that they've never seen before.

CLEAR GOALS

Great leadership is hard, but, fortunately, it is, to a great extent, a learnable skill, and through daily practice, one can become more, do more and have more.

During crises, such as the current global pandemic, business owners need, more than ever, to focus and have their business recovery plan as a first priority. For this to happen successfully, there is a true need for clear and specific goals that will lead them back to success.

In the *Born to Win* book and programme by the legendary icon of motivational and inspirational speaking, Zig Ziglar, and my very good friend and brother, Tom Ziglar, it is clear that when there is hope for change and a plan for that to happen, one can increase their chances of winning and becoming successful. In order to win, one has to plan to win, prepare to win and expect to win; hope is the catalyst that will get everything started and encouragement keeps it alive.

> *Encouragement is the fuel on which hope runs.*
> Zig Ziglar

Having clear goals can be the first steps a leader can take towards securing a successful business re-bounce.

The seven steps of goal setting, according to *Born To Win*, can be summarised as following:

1. Identifying a goal, writing it down and describing it clearly, as without identifying a clear target, we aim nowhere. Here is one of my favourite heroic and heart-warming examples that relates to an important target: It was that specific goal, and the clear target of having planet Earth (Home) in sight in that small triangle window of the Apollo 13 spacecraft, that helped NASA astronaut and commander Capt. Jim Lovell bring the crew safely home in April 1970. The desire was there, to come back home; all they needed was to see the target, even for a short while, while performing a series of corrective turns to direct the spacecraft towards the target, Earth. They did it, and all because of a clear and specific goal.

2. List the benefits of achieving that goal, making sure there is a clear and specific list of why achieving the goal is so important. Is it to bring the business back to what it was before? Is it for personal pride? Is it so that everyone can have their jobs while the business is also thriving? What are the benefits of becoming successful again?

3. Obstacles to overcome in achieving the goal. As a business leader, and together with the team, making a list of clear and anticipated obstacles can only add to the degree of preparation needed to achieve the goal.

4. Leadership can be lonely, as people try to figure out things by themselves, but, sometimes, asking around for help from friends and team members can enrich the experience and lead to clearer choices and results.

5. Listing the skills and knowledge required to achieve goals is very important for utilising the proper resources, especially in time of crisis, as resources can be scarce. A powerful combination of knowledge and skills is needed to successfully achieve goals.

6. Identifying key people and groups to work with. This goes back to communication and sharing goals with key people in order to get their input and help, thus leading to better results. Together, people can achieve more. A good business leader will communicate the vision and the strategies ahead with everyone, while also finding key people who can accelerate the process to achieving these goals.

7. Developing a plan of action. It seems obvious that if there is a goal in mind, there should be a plan of action for following it, but people can talk themselves out of achieving their goals simply by not implementing it. This is the most critical step, according to *Born To Win*, as it involves thinking through the details of how to achieve a specific goal. This could mean breaking down a big goal into smaller, bite-sized goals that can be achieved more easily and in increments, with the compound effect being achieving the bigger goal.

8. Setting a deadline for achieving a goal. A leader cannot have an endless goal in mind, as this will confuse everyone, and

will prove difficult to measure. Success can be measured by one metric or another; for success to happen, goals and action plans are needed, but they also need to be attached to a timeline or a metric, so that when achieved (even if it is in stages or phases), people know they have achieved them and become more enthusiastic and capable of moving to the next phase.

Zig Ziglar famously said you have to *be* before you can *do*, and you have to *do* before you can *have*!

Becoming a successful master '*goal setter*' is the process of being the person and leader one needs to be, and by doing what has to be done in order to change an organisation and make the world a better place. It all starts from within and from what your vision is in life.

In life (which includes your business), your goals and missions can lead in the same direction without you even thinking about it.

One of the top coaches in the world and a magnificent influencer and mentor, Jack Canfield, co-creator of the *New York Times* bestseller, the Chicken Soup for the Soul" series, and co-author of *The Success Principles: How to Get from Where You Are to Where You Want to Be,* mentions in his super-action plan, 'The Success Principles Workbook,' that you have to take 100 percent responsibility for your life, and to be clear 'why' you are here and why you do what you do.

What is your life's purpose? Because only when you know this can you decide what you want in life.

Jack highlights the power of goal setting to achieve your vision in life; if you have no vision in life, how could you expect a vision for your business?

In his action-plan book, 'The Success Principles Workbook,' Jack stresses that it is up to us as individuals to practice what it takes to create success. Whether success is having more money, more fulfilling relationships, enjoying life more by having more time or making a greater difference in the world is all up to us. He goes on by saying that he can only provide you with a practical plan for implementing these life-changing principles and making them into a habit for the rest of your life.

The same applies here for the advice and plans in this book. It is your role, your mission, to implement what is being presented here. Obviously, most of the action plans in this book are designed in a manner that is easy to understand, follow and implement. It is a success cookbook recipe that you cannot miss, and is easy to implement with the right mental attitude and appetite for success.

PART FOUR

GETTING STARTED WITH YOUR NEW PLANS

Getting your business across the bridge of recovery means a lot of new ways of thinking and finding innovative ways to conduct business like you have never done before. We see offline businesses trying to go online, and online businesses trying to find new ways to dominate their share of the market.

Professional service-type businesses are finding new ways to communicate with their customers via tele-meetings and other forms of communication.

Navigating a business through this pandemic crisis, as mentioned before, requires new skills and a willingness to make changes.

Making sure there is an understanding of the various phases of recovery, and that each phase is recovery, regardless of the length of time it may take, and being able to plan and distinguish the transitions between these phases is important for business metric analysis and, very importantly, for overall morale.

BEING PREPARED AND INFORMED

❖ As information is changing hourly, staying ahead of the information and gathering data on daily basis can allow us to gain a better perspective to make judgements and decisions.

❖ Use the gained information, with help of experts and consultants, to reach better decisions. You know your business very well, perhaps more than anyone else. However, a consultant and an expert in business recovery may know few more things that you overlooked and could help you find a shorter route to recovery.

❖ Distinguish between hard facts, soft facts and speculations, and question everything you see and hear, especially through the media, as they never show the big picture, but rather what is happening at a particular moment in time.

❖ Stay in touch with employees and staff members and keep their knowledge and information current. They need to know what the business leader is thinking, even if the information is minimal. Business owners/leaders should not assume that, just because they follow the latest information regarding their business recovery, their staff knew it too. That is the role of a leader: to inform, stay in control and positive and plan the recovery, possibly with their input.

❖ Avoid a slow and cumbersome process of making tactical decisions by assembling a number of team members who have proved trusted in the past to come up with these tactical decisions, knowing that nothing is 'set in stone,' but rather moving with time and the information available. It is better to be flexible in these times; if new information dictates to change rapidly, then change rapidly. Working and collaborating on digital platforms make these rapid updates happen more efficiently.

❖ Understand that everyone in your team is anxious, including yourself; thus, an honest and transparent level of communication and collaboration is crucial. Going above and beyond for your team members and their needs can only result in better performance and loyalty, which is the most important ingredient in a recovery.

❖ If team members need / can work remotely, as a business leader, you need to make it very clear what that involves and how they can do it in the best possible way. If time remuneration is adjusted accordingly, explain why and how you reached the decision. People like and want clarity.

THE FOUR BUSINESS RECOVERY STAGES

1. The current situation: Any activity or movement, even the slightest, can be part of the initial phase of getting out of the situation slowly. It is all about planning. As the saying goes, failing to plan is planning to fail. It is not about going back to work and starting from where we left it; in fact, we will be starting from a negative position.

2. Pre-recovery (The official starting phase): This is when we realise that business is NOT as usual and it will not be for some time. What do we need to do when business is not conforming to usual norms? What are the strategies and steps one has to take in order to bounce back successfully?

3. The recovery (itself): All the business figures and metrics will be all over the chart. How to plan and deal with this will be a true challenge, but when we have the right plans in place, this stage, which could take up to six to twelve months, can move quicker and smoother. Any proper and rapid plans can create a significant shortcut to effective recovery.

4. The Post-Recovery: The maintenance phase, which is extremely important and can take up to a year, and, for some, even longer. This is where your plans and actions will put you in a strong maintenance position, to prepare for the future if the economy is hit again for any reason.

It is important to face the reality that recovery is a journey and a process that will not happen fast. For some, depending on their market, this may be faster or slower than for others.

The important matter is to be on the fastest track in general recovery, while also making sure you are on the fastest track for your market. Your business does not and cannot outrun the pandemic, or any other crisis for that matter, but it needs to outrun any competition in the same market. The survival and thriving of your business depends on the next steps and moves that you make as business owner and leader.

TIME MANAGEMENT AND SUCCESS

THE BEST NINE STEPS TO MANAGE YOUR TIME EFFICIENTLY!

The reason we're talking about time management here, which seems like we're talking about the obvious, is because since 'business is not as usual,' and we have to set new goals and ways to focus on these goals, a very important ingredient will be implementation, as mentioned.

> THINGS WHICH MATTER MOST MUST NEVER BE AT THE MERCY OF THINGS WHICH MATTER LEAST.
>
> GOETHE

All those things, from goal-setting to planning to implementation, require time management, as time is the one thing that we don't have much of, at least at this stage of the recovery.

Every minute counts as we come out of this hibernation into action. You need to move fast in order to deliver fast results for a fast recovery; therefore, time management is essential.

As a business owner and leader, you are under pressure most of the time; there is never enough time to do everything you want, from dedicating enough time to the business itself, or to spending valuable time with loved ones—until recently, when almost everyone was forced, one way or another, to stay home because of the current pandemic crisis. All of a sudden, people had time, and perhaps too much of it. Many had to reevaluate what is and is not important in life.

Time is the one thing that we get only once, and we never get it back.

Now, as businesses are slowly reopening, there is this urge to do a lot in a short period of time. We went from having all the time in the world to rushing again to get ready to work. Time remained constant, but our situations changed.

Businesses need to get ready again, and governments are realising that there is a need for new rules and regulations (depending on the type of business) to safeguard consumers and employees alike.

New regulatory directives are announced almost every day; thus, business owners find themselves in a rush, trying to do too many things in a short time so that they can keep their businesses going. In this short period of time, they can only do so much, and prioritise a few things only. Now, more than ever, there is a real need to master time management.

At a glance, it seems like there's plenty of time, but the reality is that time is of the essence now. Since some recovery actions require the involvement of others, from surveying and planning a safe environment, to servicing equipment that stopped working since March, other people are also running around to cope with demand and get businesses back on track. Therefore, there's a desperate need to manage our days in the most efficient way possible.

By now, you should know your priorities. You have put plans together for a speedy recovery and dedicated the time and focus to start implementing the most important elements to get the business back on track.

For all that to happen, you need to utilise your time wisely, as once it disappears, it's gone for good.

If you do not decide what you want to do with your time, it will be decided for you. Therefore, make sure you have a plan for every day in advance, based on the goals and the actions you want to take on that day. Ideally, before your day finishes, you want to plan the following day, so that it is in your subconscious for the following day. This will increase efficiency and productivity like you have never seen before, because when the new day starts, you already know what the most important tasks are to do and in what order, and that makes you on top of everything.

Remember, we discussed the topic of focusing on your goals and plans by picking up only what matters the most at any one time. This will potentially increase your efficiency and focus, as focus and time go hand in hand together, and, as they say, 'dailing to plan is planning to fail.'

Your businesses recovery depends on your time management. Since, at the moment and for the unforeseeable future, nothing seems to be as usual, your time management also shouldn't be like before. Carrying on using your time like you did before can only have damaging consequences for your business. This is a time to step up your game by not allowing any wastage, especially when it is something so precious as time.

You cannot prioritise if you don't know your priorities.
D. Abdah

ORGANISE YOUR TIME AROUND YOUR PRIORITIES

Anything that is not a priority, or is at the bottom of your list, you should put aside for now; otherwise, it will eat into your day and take up your focus, clouding your mind.

Make sure people around you are aware of that and respect it, so they do not waste your time with trivial things.

Defend your time and boundaries with all you've got. This world is full of people who will happily waste your time on meaningless things that don't matter to anyone.

Make sure that never happens to you!

Encourage a sense of focus and sharp time management in your team, so that they use their time wisely to increase efficiency and productivity. This way, they will also respect your time even more and try not to waste it.

Stephen Covey described in the bestselling book, *The Seven Habits of Highly Effective People*, the notion, or, as he calls it, habit of putting first things first.

Successful people share one common thing, and it's not hard work, good luck or human relations, but giving priority to things that matter by putting first things first. They do things that others don't like doing; that is one of the major differences between highly effective and successful people and others.

Effective people have different methods for guarding their time, using their time and dedicating it to daily tasks.

Some prefer single-item lists (like most people do); others prefer groups or chunks based on the type of activities, or having two columns for urgent and non-urgent. That way, it can be part of the daily plan, with visual clues as a guide.

We have to look at matters by how important or how urgent they are.

Some things are urgent, other things are important but not urgent, and certain things are both important and urgent; focusing on these can be a time saver and get things done faster.

Also, as part of time management, we need to learn to say 'no' more often, because when we are back at work, most everyone will want a piece of you, from employees and co-workers to customers and clients, and some of these things will take up lot of your valuable time without adding any value to your day or business.

Therefore, like every good leader, we need to learn how to say 'no!'

NINE STEPS FOR BETTER TIME MANAGEMENT

1. Know what you spend your time on. Know how you spend your time. Dedicate a slot to the method you are using to spend this time.

2. Find out what you want to spend time on in your priority list. It's crucial to prioritise.

    Sometimes, it is hard to know how to prioritise when everything seems to be a priority, as there will be days where every single task is important, and every single task appears to be urgent. However, even at times when everything seems urgent, there is an order to that urgency. Is it in order of appearance? Or the order of final results?

    You need to become skilled at separating the top three priorities from a long list of priorities. Practice is your best chance to get the skills needed.

3. You can use the humble 'pen and paper' or use planning tools, such as planning apps and software. They will help you tremendously in organising and visualising your tasks.

4. Get organised about using the time slots for what you intended to use them for.

5. Schedule your time appropriately. Certain matters need more time than others, so be mindful how much time you spend on each task. It's up to you how you divide that chunk of time you have. Just remember that you only have one chunk of time at any one time, so use it wisely. That time slot will never come back.

6. Delegate as much as you can to people you trust to do the job properly. This way, you don't have to spend all your time on every single task. There are people around you who can do these tasks and are happy to do it for you. This will also empower them and make them feel valuable and trusted.

7. Stop procrastinating and finding excuses not to do things. This is, by far, the number one enemy of progress. Attach a negative mental connotation to procrastination so that you avoid it at all costs.

8. Manage time-wasting tasks and don't let them eat into your schedule.

9. Despite all the urgency and importance of the tasks, try not to make your day and your diary be rigid and restricted. Don't forget to enjoy spontaneous moments, develop rich human interactions and have fun.

It's important to realise that there will be challenges in time management, and that you need to always encourage yourself. Remember, as a leader, there is no one out there to encourage you to stay on task and on target except you, because they are all waiting for you to perform as a leader, and that is what leaders do: They lead!

Life is full of distractions, and if we feel like something is not fun, our minds will find ways to procrastinate and find all kinds of reasons not to do it, so be careful about the challenges ahead.

When you are trying to plan something, and the challenges seem overwhelming, your mind will try to steer in the direction of procrastination, as it seems more fun not to do things, resulting in you going back to things that don't matter, but you do anyway just because it makes you feel better. You always find yourself in a reactive mode; you need to master time management, as time management itself can be a challenge for some, and it needs mastering in order to become more effective and productive. During this time of recovery, you cannot afford to be slack with your time management.

Sometimes, in the beginning, you will be distracted, but keep reminding and encouraging yourself, and visualise the end results and the satisfaction and self-respect you will get out of it.

Sometimes you may need to force yourself and teach yourself to stick to it and be on target. The same way leadership is a skill that can be learned, and which later could become part of a personality, time management also can be practised, mastered and become one of your worthy habits, leading you and your organisation and business to be more productive and efficient, and ultimately more successful.

If you want to thrive, you need to master this as one of the pillars of successful leadership.

PART FIVE

THE RESILIENT LEADER

During stable times, most businesses are supposed to run smoothly, without major or sudden surprises. Therefore, even a mediocre leader can go unnoticed by employees and customers, as the business is just ticking on nicely, life-changing decisions are usually not required and every day is more or less like the day before.

However, in challenging and dynamic times, resilience can make the difference between a merely surviving business or a thriving one.

One of the characteristics of a resilient leader is the ability to be responsive to crisis. In order for a response to be efficient and effective, there are certain elements that it needs to display, such as having access to extra production capacity and channels of fulfilment, as these will make the business more flexible, thus letting it adjust better in the face of crisis. Being able to rearrange supplies (if one supplier is down, another one can step in fast and deliver parts or services that are needed) is essential for the continuity of the business.

In 2018, most KFC fast food restaurants in the UK came to a grinding halt for a short while. They could not have their main ingredient, chicken meat, delivered because of some issues in distribution and operations. Until a new supply channel was established, the company lost a lot of revenue and customers, who moved to rivals, such as McDonald's and Burger King, despite the products not being exactly the same. This supply chain incident demonstrated the vulnerability of any sort business, even a conglomerate like KFC, if there is no immediate redundancy plan.

Any business could face that, but the smaller the business niche, the more dramatic and negative the effects will be. If a particular business allows for diversifying its activities and production, it may have a better chance of surviving crisis. An example of a resilient system is McDonald's. They have a diverse selection of fast food products, made in a very systematic and certain way, making it a systems-dependent business rather than a people-dependent business. This is why the chain has been replicated successfully around the world, each location giving the same look and feel down to the smallest detail.

According to Michael Gerber, the author the successful The E-Myth series, each business needs systems—perhaps not to the extent of a franchise, such as McDonald's, but all require a system of some sort. He calls it the Business Development process. If a business has no systems in place, the outcome can be tragic. However, if this process is done right by any small to medium business owner, the result can be a bulletproof and predictable system for success that could be repeated for any business.

The current crisis has resulted in some business owners wishing they had other businesses in other sectors, or at least other services and products in the same sector; if one temporarily stopped, the other could carry on. This is why having a modular business, especially in crises and challenging times, can prove more effective than traditional highly integrated systems, which may be quite efficient until crisis happens and the system stops or collapses.

The best resilient systems need to be evolving all the time if they want to deal with opportunities and problems, such as the current pandemic crisis. An evolved and responsive system can adapt much quicker to the necessary changes that the new post-pandemic world commands. Waiting for a crisis to pass completely might sound like a wise choice, but it could also be too late for the businesses who did not want to adapt to the new world. Being responsive and doing something, even just a little, is a good strategy, at least for now.

The level of uncertainty is at its highest for this generation. As a business owner, managing to envision downturn and hardship scenarios as part of a simulated assessment to test the systems of the business is very important for planning to prevent future financial and logistic problems. Many companies had a very abrupt stop without any contingency plans, leading many thousands of businesses owners to seek help, applying for government loans and aid in order to survive until it is safe to resume activities. If they'd had a contingency plan in place, at least financially, the effect of hardship would have been more tolerable in the short term.

Companies need to be vigilant now and take a good look at future potential disaster scenarios, putting a plan together to help themselves and others, at least in the short term. This is what we are trying to achieve in this book, among other things to help business owners.

A resilient system is also a system that is part of the 'big socio-economic picture,' creating trust and partnership between all parties: customers, teams, supply chains and other partners. This is a time for unity, for reaching out and helping one another, as one business thriving at the expense of others is unacceptable in these times of crisis. We all have a moral obligation towards our fellow human beings; this is no time for 'jungle-survival skills.'

Another attribute of a resilient system is to be prepared for future problems and crisis, anticipating the road ahead. The percussion of this pandemic could affect our lives and businesses in unexpected ways for years to come; being prepared for future potential disasters is key for being resilient and ahead of the game.

One such preparation is running or simulating scenarios to measure how prepared your team is to deal with future downturns in the light of available information. How we behave under stress is crucial for such a drill, so this may require a small group of dedicated team members who are specifically trained and have the intellectual power to function well under stress.

This epidemic can be used as a valuable learning opportunity. Every step taken to remedy the business in recovery should be well documented and studied later to extract valuable lessons for the future. Leaning to use tools, such as SWOT analysis, in the light of this crisis, and noting how we behaved and acted upon certain matters or how we reached certain decisions, could become life lessons, preparing us for the future and the unknown. Mistakes will happen, but the important thing is that we should always learn from them, using the new intelligence to propel us into the future.

NASA did not give up as soon as they faced a setback or a disaster, even as dramatic and tragic as some of these setbacks were. There was a main goal and a mission that had to be reached; that is what businesses need. Any information is good information when we act upon it to improve something.

Human existence on this beautiful planet of ours is full of amazing and encouraging stories of human resilience and conquer. Conquering, adapting and defeating failure is 'our' specialty as humans, and no epidemic or disaster can take away that from us. Collectively, we can achieve and aim for the impossible; history is full of examples.

It is all about believing in ourselves and modelling others who have done it before us. There is no shame in learning from others and modelling yourself after successful examples in life.

Just showing up on Monday morning and watching the business ticking along is no longer acceptable. Business owners who, in the past, never bothered to learn enough financial skills will pay a hefty price from now on. The world of full of great advice and mentors, and, today, any skill can be easily taught at a click of a button, so try to learn finance, marketing, management and other important skills. In the end, you will become better informed regarding many aspects that relate to your business; this will ultimately make you a better leader. No one likes to work with, or for, an ignorant leader.

Ignorance, especially in this era and the future post-pandemic era, is intellectual and business suicide. This is why you are still reading this book. We want to be different and make a difference. As a result, in this enlightening process, we may change ourselves, our businesses and, hopefully, the world around us.

A big congratulations to you!

PART SIX

HOW MANY ASPECTS OF THE BUSINESS NEED CHANGING IN ORDER TO THRIVE?

The simple answer to this question is: as many things as it takes! There are no set rules, or a one-size-fits-all method, or a global formula. Each business is unique. However, most businesses of the same size or in the same market share some commonalities, which we are about to discuss. Changing even one little thing in each sector can create a compound effect, causing a positive ripple effect.

It is important to realise the various stages of recovery action. At the very first stage of recovery, we may not need to do certain things, which may become very handy later. As mentioned before, these steps and actions are all important, but must take place at different intervals, and every business needs to adjust them according to their unique situation and position.

SAFETY FIRST

We must first sure it is safe for ourselves, team members, employees and the public to conduct and resume activities, perhaps not like before, but in a new, adaptive way that conforms to the laws of the country and, most importantly, to ethical and legal common sense.

By now, most businesses around the world have been following some legal, ethical governing body's requirements for safety first—or, at least, one hopes so. Remember, not everyone is informed the same way, although it may look like it. Not everyone is a virologist or epidemiologist, and people exhibit different understanding of phrases such as 'social distancing' and the like.

Some businesses, employees or members of the public (customers, clients) may behave in an erratic way towards the new norms; in their mind, it is business as usual post-lockdown. However, one hopes that most people are at a level of intelligence to know that this threat to humanity is real, and that one should take it seriously and not in an ignorant manner. As business leaders and team members, it is our duty to set the parameters for our activities and explain to our beloved clients what is and what is not acceptable in the most respectful way.

We have all had the opportunity to go out to run important errands; while doing this, we could notice the variations in the responses of some outlets, and how safe or unsafe they are. Some are very pragmatic and deal with it in an efficient but safe manner, while others made it difficult, to the extent of making customers feel guilty for being there, somehow alienating customers with the way they were treated. This comes from panic and misunderstanding; certain actions seem acceptable and others not, and yet, the reality could be exactly the opposite. This usually happens in larger outlets, such as supermarkets and DIY stores, where you could feel bad or guilty if you walked against the direction of the arrows painted on the floor.

Try to be vigilant and create a safe environment, but without disrespecting others and making them feel as if they just landed on the planet. A reliable system does not mean a discriminating system.

Initially, start with your team members and employees, making sure that their welfare is your most urgent concern, that the environment they are in is adequately safe and that you have done everything in your power to give them the reassurance they need to function in a safe environment. This may require rethinking the way things were done before, making sure everyone understands the new norms and why it is important to do it the new way.

COMMUNICATION SKILLS

In the current crisis, people and the media are using many scary words, such as pandemic, epidemic, apocalypse and global crisis, and while most of these terms are merely describing certain aspects of the current crisis, they all sound very scary to everyone.

Earlier in this book, we looked at the way people behave during crisis; some are more positive than others, with some being so scared that they become almost paralysed, not knowing what to do in the face of a threat like this. This person could be your employee, or even a family member.

How you deal with that?

We also mentioned earlier that we cannot put one method of information over all our employees, regardless of their level of fear, hoping that they all take it in the same way.

Clearly, in these situations, it is best to be honest about the threats you are facing, and to tell employees how much you know, while not pretending that you have everything under control or giving false hope.

You need to communicate in such a manner that things are clear and honest, but, at the same time, not blown out of proportion. People generally listen to bad news and exaggeration, so don't enable that.

Talk to your employees without using absolute statements, such as 'never' or 'always.' Just be honest and don't give false hope.

As a leader, it is your responsibility to choose your words and your tone very carefully, making sure that you don't downplay any threats or danger, while at the same time not scaring people constantly by using scary words in such a tone that employees have no choice but to shut down, become uncertain and lose all hope.

Your job as a leader is to inspire your people, not to scare them. Give a positive spin on most things you say and choose your words carefully.

Your business is your ship, and you need to steer the ship in the right direction and in the right manner.

Do not use big words, like the ones used by government agencies and authorities, which can make people even more confused.

Your employees and team members have been with you for a while; they know you, and they know how you talk and behave. Don't try to be dishonest with them in downplaying or overplaying anything, because they will recognise the tonality, and they will know if you have been telling the truth or not.

When you know someone very well, and you work for or with them for a while, you can even hear them saying something in the tone of their voice, without needing any words; this is what some call 'reading between the lines.' This is definitely not the time for letting people second-guess what you say by trying to read between the lines.

Be direct, straight to the point and decisive.

Show your understanding for their fears. Show them that you're on their side, and that we are all in this together.

You need to communicate genuinely and tell them about how you feel as an individual, not necessarily as the business owner; that way, they see that what has affected them also affected you. Remind them that you are all in this together.

Make your employees understand that if there is a new situation that they don't understand or do not know how to deal with, it's fine, and that you are all working together, navigating these difficult times in order to make things better.

It is best, in time of crisis, to show leadership, asking for certain things to be done in certain ways for the safety of the public and employees. However, it's also good practise to make sure that the employees buy into these changes, and you need to invite their input on how things could be improved. When everyone is involved, it makes them feel a shared ownership, hopefully leading to better results.

Set up direct channels for communication, whether it's physically being there while respecting social distancing, or by means of online meetings. Whichever way you decide, make sure you have an exchange platform and a Q&A platform that people can use to ask questions relating to everything that relates to their jobs and roles. Try to answer them publically so that everyone can see, creating a culture of transparency where the information is out there for all your employees.

During the lockdown, some companies have managed to keep in touch online; they have also managed to have coffee breaks and lunch breaks together online, which can be a very good, positive experience for everyone. A few companies have gone further and arranged for 'Friday nights out' together online, where they can all meet on one of the online platforms and just be casual. They may not be talking about work, but this way they feel they still belong together, and that they can still have a good time despite the lockdown. These are very clever, innovative ways of keeping people together, which is good for them psychologically.

During crisis, perhaps even more so now, try to create a culture of being there for each other. Turn it into a ritual that makes people appreciate the fact that you appreciate them; they will be proud of the type of business they are working for. This shows that this is not just any company, but a company with a mission involving their people, encouraging them to look out for each other.

Looking after each other has never proven more important in our lifetime than now.

As a business owner and the leader of your team, as mentioned before, you need to be transparent and honest. However, you also need to know what you communicate and with whom, because different people can handle different information in different ways. Although we encourage transparency with everyone, certain aspects of the business might apply to some employees more than others, and it is not good to tell or burden everyone with it. Some employees, depending on their role and position, may need more specific details or data than everyone else. Therefore, while still maintaining integrity and honesty with the rest, a particular team member may be given more information as needed to move things forward.

If the information involves lots of data that may not be relevant, it may scare and overwhelm them. So, choose your words, tonality and whom you talk to and about what carefully, as things can get lost in translation in larger groups.

If, during the crisis, you had a successful online communication channel with your employees, maybe you should carry on doing so in the future. Instead of bringing people back only to meet up for few hours, they could do it from the comfort of their homes; the time otherwise spent commuting could be spent on something useful for the business, and they will appreciate that.

With regards to your customers and clients, if you already had some channels of communication, this is a good time to ask them what they need, see how they would like to be helped and show your human side to them. Show them that you are just like them, and that you live the same experience as everyone; however, always keep it professional and do not over-promise anything.

If they need your services and products, try communicating clearly with them regarding timing and style of delivery. See if you can help in any way; that way, it shows them that you are trustworthy and that you are there for them.

If you didn't have any channels of communication, maybe this is a good time to create channels, like additional mailings or publishing podcasts, video conferences, video messages, consultations or webinars.

For example, if you have a new service or a new product, you can create a webinar and invite your customers to come and have a look; that way, you show that you care by trying to save them the journey and keeping them safe, while at the same time reminding them that you are there now, and that you have a new service or product that may be of help. You could start your communication just by simply saying, 'We're here for you. We prepared this video for you, so please have a look.'

Most clients will appreciate that you are thinking of them in this time of crisis, especially if, in your products or services, there is more for them to gain personally than you just trying to make a sale.

Make sure your communication is simple and straight to the point, perhaps providing some tips and things they can do straight away to implement it. Make it easy to remember, because if it's easy to remember, they will probably tell others to join your channel.

Remember that people will remember which companies were there for them during the crisis and which companies turned their backs.

As businesses, as we know business will probably take a different shape in the future. One of those areas that may affect your business in the future will be how we communicate with our clients.

Nowadays, there are online consultations for doctors and patients; there are contactless vehicle deliveries and many other remote or contactless services; and nobody can be sure that everything will ever go back to exactly where it was before the pandemic crisis. Certain things will probably go back to normality but rest assured that there will be aspects of business that will take a different shape permanently. We have to realise that and be prepared for it, because whoever is prepared now will reap the benefits in the future.

DECISION MAKING

It is clear during times of crisis that our ability to make rational choices may somehow be altered. All of our lives have been turned upside down for some time now. Nothing appears to be the way it used to be. But, this is exactly where, paradoxical as it may seem, there is positive opportunity: conscious reorientation.

> *Difficult times let us develop determination and inner strength.*
> Dalai Lama

Decision-making can be difficult at times like this, so you are not the only one who might be indecisive at times under the current pandemic pressure. Entire nations and countries are facing threats; even governments can't decide on one thing or another. So if you can't decide on something straight away. don't beat yourself up. It is part of our DNA to pay attention to threats; we are just wired that way. Perhaps spending time reflecting on solutions is not a bad idea, hence the many strategies and plans in this book to help you in your decision making.

People can make wrong, irrational choices in the face of uncertainty, such as selling their stocks and shares in the face of fear, thinking acting quickly is the answer, while the opposite could be more sensible. A rushed decision, based on fear, is almost never a good thing to do; slowing down and reflecting could be the route to better decision making.

As a leader, practising patience and slowing down while facing the decision-making process can prove vital for the steps and results that follow the decision. Taking the time to analyse data and facts, looking at possible scenarios and how to act in each scenario, reasoning with the pros and cons of a decision and allowing for time to digest all that, and sometimes even delaying the decision all together, can prove far more beneficial than irrational, fast-acting choices in the face of a threat.

Just because you are the owner of a business or a leader doesn't mean you are under an obligation to make fast decisions all the time. Fast decisions can be of essence sometimes, when all the facts are present, but not always, whereas slowing down is the right choice most of the time.

Inaction can be an art in itself. Not many people can master it, but, when they do, and know how and when to do it, it can be very effective. However, this shouldn't become a habit, as not all situations require a long period of reflection or inaction. It is only to be used in certain situations, such as when it is better to wait for further information and facts. Researchers indicate that leaders who mastered inaction also know when to make a fast decision if they have all the data they need, because, when you slow down your decision-making process, you also become more observant, allowing yourself to judge and analyse the situation better, so that when the opportunity comes, you know when to act fast.

It has been said that in times of existential crisis, such as the current pandemic, it is best not to base your decisions on gut feeling, but rather to slow down and take the time necessary to make better choices. Fast decisions may lead to a temporary victory over your anxiety, but may cause bigger problems later.

Exceptional situations require reflection on the essentials. In order to keep ourselves mentally afloat and waste less energy being upset about small things, we must reorganise our priorities, return to our principles, learn again to recognise and express our own needs and to express the life we had before the crisis. Since we are actually doing better than at the start of the pandemic, surprisingly, this makes our view of what we really want clearer. We are far less distracted by trivialities in the decisions that we are now making; in view of what threatens life, we have become more confident and determined in our wishes. This increases the quality of our decisions enormously! If we manage to control our feelings of anxiety, fear, uncertainty and concern, and we don't allow ourselves to be flooded with the negative, a crisis could be a time when we can make particularly good decisions.

OLD HABITS

They say old habits die hard, but that doesn't mean they cannot be fixed or changed.

For whatever reason, if you recognise that there are some old habits in your organisation that stop or hinder you from achieving your goals, there is a solution for that!

Unless your entire model is based online, most traditional businesses suffered one way or another due the pandemic crisis. It wasn't so much because there was something wrong with the business model, but because no one had anticipated the aftermath of this pandemic.

Even governments, with all their mighty departments, were not ready, so how could a small business have been?

The lack of customer traffic to the business was one of the main factors, due to lockdowns and the fear of going out. Another main reason was also the lack of supplies, as most parts of the world stopped functioning.

We all know a few successful restaurants, we all know successful car dealerships and we all know many successful brick-and-mortar businesses; however, these are only as successful as the customer traffic they have.

The problem is, when these businesses had to shut down, whether or not they had enough contingency plans to survive the lockdown financially.

Many businesses had to resort to government help and bank loans just to keep paying bills until they re-opened.

If businesses had contingency plans, and, in an ideal world, anywhere from three, six or twelve months of cash reserves, most would have been fine for a while.

If they didn't have any contingency cash reserves or other plans set aside for a day like this, those businesses probably have suffered the most. Some businesses, while not making money and having no revenue, had to borrow even more money in order to survive, or to bring their technologies up to speed for after the pandemic, such as making sure that customers are safe when they reopen. Many had to invest in antiviral machines, or special air ventilation technologies, for example.

If you were one of those unfortunate businesses who had no contingency plans, you need to look at the historical data of your company and see why that happened. Usually, it's because of some old habits of doing things.

Some companies, while they were enjoying a good revenue, were used to spending it fast. Fast and high spending levels usually prevent a business from being able to have a cash reserve for a rainy day. These matters can be part of a business culture, the bad old habits that need changing. This is a good time to review yourself, your priorities and some of the old ways you used to run your business.

Honesty is the key here, and since you are not sharing this with anyone, at least you could be honest with yourself and see what your shortcomings are that led to this, if you are part of this category.

When you look at your business on the day of the lockdown, when the company's revenue stopped coming in, but just before that, your business was running on an overdraft with the help of multiple credit cards, then you had a big problem regardless of the pandemic's affect on your business.

So, was it the way you were running your business, or was it some external factors that led to that over the years, or was it even both?

Either way, something was fundamentally wrong with the way the business was running. Bearing in mind that is not always the fault of the business owner, as there might have been some external factors that played a role, however, for the majority of cases, these kinds of things don't happen overnight, and therefore a large portion of the responsibility is usually placed on the business owner.

Normally, if something doesn't work, you fix it; so if, as a business owner, this has been a problem for years, and you were just hoping that, one day, it would go away, that was a big mistake.

A problem like this probably has been brewing for some time. Perhaps the pandemic was only the last straw, and not the reason why there is no cash reserve.

As business owners, we have all made mistakes, and we have all been in situations where we could have done much better, or acted wiser and smarter. That's called life, and we learn from it.

The question is: Do we continue in that path, or do we want to do something about it?

As a business owner, you may realise there are some old habits that led to this situation, such as not paying enough attention to the company's financial metrics on a daily or weekly basis, or perhaps having a wrong marketing strategy, or dedicating a lot of resources towards investments and technology that probably didn't serve your business in the best way, or perhaps just taking a finger off the pulse of your business for a while.

If you relate to any of these issues, then you are not alone. The good news is that this is a good time to fix it, especially if you know how to fix it.

However, if you know what the problems are but you don't know how to solve them, then perhaps this is a time to either educate yourself and find out about solutions, or perhaps consider working with a business consultant or a mentor who can help.

Don't forget that, whether you have one or multiple businesses, that's your world and your bubble; having a consultant or a mentor might be a good idea, as they have helped other businesses. Most of them are very knowledgeable and smart about picking up the obvious and the not-so-obvious problems the business or you, as a leader of the business, may have.

Instead of you spending valuable time figuring out things and trying to fix everything by yourself, maybe one of the best investments you make is hiring a consultant to look at the business with a fresh set of eyes, coming up with solutions and holding you accountable to implement those solutions, or maybe even helping you with implementation.

Today, we have many business coaches, consultants and business gurus out there, ready to help. Some will even help you implement the changes and follow up with you until you are standing on your feet and becoming very successful. Others are happy to share their knowledge with you, draw a plan and give you the route, but you have to implement it by yourself.

You need first to recognise your need; only you know whether you need help or not. You have to decide whether you want to rebuild your empire and put that fire in your belly once again, like when you started your business all those years ago.

You should learn all the new skills and new ways of doing things, which might be different from when you first started, or you can allow someone, like a business consultant with a good reputation who understands your type of business, to help you change these old habits. As we said, old habits die hard, but they are not impossible to change or fix.

Sometimes, knowing or sensing that something is wrong in the business can be easy, but trying to figure out 'what' is exactly wrong might be more difficult, and that's why others may see it better than yourself.

Often, in the small business environment, people think the business is them, and they are the business, which can be wrong.

Yes, you need to brand yourself as part of the business, but you are not your business. Your business is merely there to serve a purpose, which is to serve you and your family, to create opportunities for others to work and have a good life and to create opportunities for customers, clients and members to benefit from your services and products. You just happen to be one part of your business, but you are not your business.

Therefore, for some business owners, when it comes to analysing their businesses, they take it very personally, which is understandable, but can blur their vision, making it hard to see what's wrong. They know something is wrong, but what that is, that's the question, and maybe only somebody from the outside world with an honest opinion can tell you that. Once you know what's wrong, then fixing it might be easier than you think.

It is like going to the doctor: If they don't have a diagnosis for your condition, they can't treat you, but once they know what is wrong, then treatment is easier and more predictable.

Owning a business is both a tremendous responsibility and joy; however, occasionally, you need to detach yourself from your business so you can think more clearly.

Look at your business from the eyes of a consultant, who doesn't share the same emotional feeling as you feel for your business. You may have inherited this business from your father, who inherited this business from his father, or you may have started the business from nothing. A consultant understands these issues, but doesn't necessarily share the emotional baggage, rather looking at what the problem is and why the business is not functioning as it should.

You can do the same, if you have the ability to detach emotionally. This skill can also be learned and mastered, but whether you want to do it or not is a different matter.

Depending on how many years you've been in business, you may have already acquired a lot of habits in the way you run your business, from personal techniques and ways of doing things that you have developed over the years (your routine), to the way you interact with clients, make calls and present your services and goods. These might all be techniques and habits, but not all habits are good, and some may need to be stopped, changed or tweaked in order to get better results.

SO, HOW DO YOU FIX YOUR OLD BAD HABITS?

1. Start by recognising the habits and fixing them one by one. It could be one bad habit that dominates everything, such as failure to implement plans. Perhaps you like every aspect about your business, except for looking at financial data, so you don't know how to analyse; that could be the one thing that is crucial to fix for your business to succeed. If you are true to yourself, you will know what that habit is once you look deeper.

2. Ask yourself and others (if you have mentors) the right type of questions. Look at the past and identify the habit. Find out where it originates from and why it was there in the first place. This way, you get to the root of the problem. Maybe it was inherited with the business when you bought it, and everyone just carried on doing the same thing over the years.

3. Make sure you make the decision about changing the habit, because identifying the habit can be easy, but owning it as a problem is another thing. Always remember that, if you find habits that need changing and they relate to the way you handle things, don't take it personally; this is no reflection on your personality, but rather just the way you have conducted certain things in certain ways. The good news is that it can be changed

4. Set a deadline for yourself and make sure you have a date by which you start to eliminate this habit. Start the process and give it priority. If there's a burning desire to change something about your leadership or about the way you conduct things, then make it your priority, because that is more important than other things, as everything else may depend on it.

Once you change a habit that's negatively affecting your business, you change it forever, and that could make a big impact on your business.

5. Try to wear the consultant hat and remember that you're good at what you do; that's why you are in business. That's why you are a leader and others respect you. Try to be your own consultant, if you can. This will make you very proud, and, in the long run, makes you able to analyse other things with a different attitude, with the view of a consultant.

6. Make sure you document everything. If you do all the thinking, analysing and finding solutions your head, you may forget vital information.

   Try to write everything down and document your progress; that way, if something doesn't work, you can trace your steps back and find a solution.

   The problem is that, if you don't document it, you may find it difficult later to recollect all that information. Therefore, from the very beginning, document what the problem is, how you identified it and what you are doing about it. Set targets, have a goal as to when you want to deal with this, measure it and go back to tweak it and finalise it, so that it becomes a technique that you can use for solving other problems in your business or, one day, helping others by becoming their consultant.

7. Do it with enthusiasm. Don't think a bad old habit is with you for the rest of your life.

   It hasn't scarred you, and it's not ingrained in you; it's just a habit, and can be changed, especially if there is a positive result attached to this change. Psychologically, this helps a lot. Therefore, show maximum enthusiasm and devotion to the change. It will pay off.

8. For every positive change you do, give yourself credit and do something that makes you feel good as a reward. This could be the simplest things, but rewarding yourself is an important psychological trigger, indicating that things are on the right track and that you are doing something to address and change an old bad habit. Remember, 'old' means in the past. The future is all yours to change and thrive in.

Only you hold the key to the future by acting with enthusiasm and dedication to change what seems like an obstacle in the way of your success.

What you've done in the past doesn't have to be what you do for the rest of your life. Always remember that!

Now, we know what to do and how it is important to make a plan as to when to do it.

Start first by setting yourself a specific time every day to deal with this. For example, for the next two weeks you will wake up one hour earlier and spend that hour looking into this.

Start your research and learn how to educate yourself on identifying these issues, then spend the next hour the following day finding solutions and planning how to implement them. Then, spend the next hour the following day implementing them, and so on.

The task can be done at any time you like, but you do need a specific time of the day, so that, mentally and psychologically, you are ready for this change. Try not to put it at the end of your long days; remember that, as your business is recovering, like most other business owners, you will be busy figuring out the health and safety issues of your customers and your employees. Plus, many other matters will be on your mind, and you will be busy with new rules and regulations for the way you conduct business. Your mind will be overwhelmed from how to repay banks and creditors, so the last thing you want at the end of your very busy day is to look at your old bad habits.

You need to be fresh. Your mind needs to be fresh and ready. You are not just solving a temporary problem in your business; this is a problem that's been with you for a while, and it deserves your maximum attention.

No one knows for sure, but maybe, one day, when all of this is over, and your business is very successful and thriving due to your dedication, hard work, excellent planning and implementation, perhaps you can guide others on how to change their old habits. Nothing brings more joy than knowing you can help someone else get out of the same problem by following these steps.

PART SEVEN

FINANCIAL FITNESS

J ust as a reminder, when we were covering other crucial aspects of business recovery, we mentioned that business owners who are not in control of their financial data risk jeopardising their businesses. Just going back on Monday morning, hoping that the business will just be ticking along nicely without you paying attention to finances is a recipe for business disaster.

Every business owner/leader should have technical knowledge regarding financial data, how to read it, what to make of it and how to use it for their advantage.

A common mistake is depending entirely on the accountant or other parties involved in looking into financial data. After all, it is your business, and you have the ultimate responsibility. You owe it to yourself and everyone around you to be knowledgeable and well-informed about your businesses' financial data. That way, you can plan and budget better solutions for your business, and, above all, decide when is a good time or not to make a purchase or scale up.

To start with, it is important to know, in all types of businesses, where revenue is coming from and where it is going, what is left (or not left) and how maximise one value while minimising another. It's just simple maths and a deep understanding of your business, but the maths principles are the same.

Make a list of the regular and occasional (but anticipated) payments you have to do. Also make note of which season is better or worse for your business, and so on. After gathering all this data, even though this is a very simple method, it will give you a bigger picture of what comes in and what goes out. Of course, there are the unexpected payments and revenue, but these could be also anticipated to an extent, based on historical business figures.

So, here is the big question: How to stay profitable?

To answer this question, we have to look at the various elements of the business financial canvas. Understanding cash flow, balance sheets, profit and loss statements, overhead costs per hour and many other aspects of the numbers and statistics for your business is crucial.

Now, let's have a look at how growth can hide unprofitability, and how a profitable business can be cash-poor and still go out of business, despite showing a high level of earnings.

The most dangerous thing for a company is very slow loss that hardly shows on financial statements. The company could be losing a few pennies for every pound, once overheads are taken into consideration, which most small business owners just guess is normal; some, tragically, don't even know it. It is a slow leakage that happens over years of financial negligence. Some will guess inventory at the end of the year for tax purposes without even taking the time to count it.

A good remedy for this problem is to take the time every month, not every quarter, to calculate and evaluate overheads and the cost of production/time services take and the actual revenue that comes in. This way, there is a constant monitoring system that allows for rapid analysis and intervention in case remedial actions need to happen.

Companies could grow, at least on paper, but not make proportional profits because the cash from one project started another one. That's why, at the end of the year, some businesses lack the cash to pay their taxes or improve their businesses, and none of them know why that is happening.

A loss in every pound or dollar, even the slightest, could go unnoticed, as it is only a tiny bit of money. Because of other pseudo-metrics in the company's finances, the business might be showing growth while, in reality, it's shrinking bit by bit. Pay attention!

One way to cover a shortage is to raise prices in general or for certain products/services, in addition to seeking professional help if the business owner feels overwhelmed and can't see a way out of the situation. It is like talking to a financial therapist! It does help.

At the bottom of any profit and loss statement, there is a value, which can be positive or negative. This is not cash; it is merely a representation of revenue and expenses, and which one exceeds the other. It is not how much you have in the bank; it is a profit or loss figure.

Profits are what you collect for a service or a product after all the expenses, and there will be months where the company shows profits yet struggles to pay its bills. Almost every company has faced a year, or more, where it showed profits but still did not have the cash to pay its taxes.

A good financial practice is to always have enough cash to cover for a six-month period if something major goes wrong, such as the current pandemic. Many businesses will re-evaluate their cash flow situations during and after recovery, and hopefully they will be prepared better in the future if anything like this happens again. We hope it never will happen again, but it may happen again, and we cannot depend on governments to bail out businesses forever, because every bailout results in increased taxes, which, in itself, affects the business.

This is the time to review accounts receivable on weekly basis and act on it, as your business depends on it like fuel.

A company's gross margin is one of the most vital elements on a financial statement and needs to be monitored monthly. This is a percentage rather than a clear number, and it is the result of gross profit (always in pounds and dollars) divided by sales. Gross margin needs to be consistent and not fluctuate too much; it may vary by a few percentage points, but no more. Every month, gross profit (in pounds and dollars) may be different, as it depends on sales volume, but the gross margin should be constant from month to month. If it's not, the following could be the reasons why:

❖ The profit and loss statement being all over the place because of someone lazy in the organisation who wants to get all the revenue figures, yet is not getting all the expenses figures. When revenues do not match the expenses incurred to produce those revenues, this problem happens. Companies who track sales without paying enough attention to the costs involved to make those sales usually suffer from the gross margin roller coaster at the end of the month. Pay attention to this, as it could be what saves your company.

❖ Ups and downs with pricing due to different salespeople selling the same products/services at different prices to customers, or if one calculates a different labour cost to entice the customer to buy.

❖ Unhappy customers and warranties, leading to remedial work, can result in extra expenses and time to fix the problem. This can lead to negative gross profit, thus affecting the gross margin. The business needs to make sure that these incidents are not happening often, as they will eat into profits very quickly.

❖ Inventory should be kept separate in the books, not in profit and loss statement, until it is needed it to produce a product; then, you can put it in cost. Otherwise, it should remain in inventory. Whenever inventory is used, there should be revenue to offset the expense.

❖ Not investigating irregularities, such as missing materials, employees leaving or staff being paid overtime to deliver a product faster while customers pay regular prices

All these things may contribute to the company's gross margin dropping, possibly by a percentage or two on monthly basis, leading to a big drop at one point, causing the business to suffer beyond repair. No business owner wants that to happen, so pay great attention to every aspect of your business' finances, especially the points mentioned above. If the gross margin is inconsistent, this is where to look for clues.

It is a dreaded time of the month, but, in the long run, you will have peace of mind and your business will thrive.

The most crucial document your business must have is a . . . PLAN!

We plan all the time. We plan our work and projects every day; we budget time and other resources for these projects. Yet, most small business owners do not have an overall plan or budget for their businesses. They just show up Monday to Friday and hope for the best to happen.

If we can plan and budget for projects, we can surely put together a few pages of useful and valuable information to plan for the year ahead. Making your operational business plan may involve many moving parts, but the most important elements of the plan are:

1. Clear goals for the business. This was covered earlier in the goal-setting section; here, we will add a few more points regarding the financial side of goal setting, especially in

the recovery stage. It is all about what you, as a business owner, want to accomplish and achieve. It is a good idea to make key employees understand the company's finances the way you see it and understand it, as that could make them understand more why certain things have to be the way they are, and what the benefits are for the company. It is not uncommon for people to leave their jobs because they feel they are just making someone else 'rich,' and that there is nothing for them in it. It is not always about the money; staff need to feel they are part of something big and worthwhile, just the way the business owner sees it. For that reason, try to set certain goals, especially financial goals, together with your team. It is surprising, how much people want to give when they are part of something worthwhile, and how they love to see the result of their common goals for the business. These should include sales goals, new customer numbers goals, gross margin goals, savings goals and, perhaps more confidentially and individually, income level and bonus goals.

YOUR GOALS MUST BE SPECIFIC, MEASURABLE & TIME LIMITED

2. How you market the business will affect the financial metrics of the business. This is about traditional marketing before the pandemic and new marketing strategies during recovery. The goal of every business is to provide a service/product and make the most profit possible in the most ethical way, which is a winwin situation for everyone. For this to happen, and for customers to come and knock your door, many forms of marketing and advertising need to happen. One of the best ways is to have a marketing cal-

endar, indicating what to do at what interval, to whom it should be directed and who is involved to make sure this happens. A simple spreadsheet can handle all this, giving up-to-the-minute information. You can also delegate certain actions to your staff or within a particular department. Very importantly, any success, small or large, should be measured and celebrated. This is crucial in this day of cash-crunch, so that you know where every penny was spent and how, and what the results were. This way, you also can an idea of what to repeat, if successful, and what not to do again, if unsuccessful.

Someone famously said that fifty percent of marketing works and the other fifty doesn't, and I wish I knew which one did work!

This means that you have to try most things that you feel are suitable for your market, and maybe occasionally even go 'wild' with new ideas. Try them and test them. But also, very importantly, measure them against results, seeing which one works and which one doesn't, repeating what worked. Always pay attention to your greatest sources of leads and nurture them.

3. Budgeting for your business and its departments. A business without budget can be like a bicycle without pedals: You have no idea how to get it into action.

Earlier, we talked about marketing and advertising as part of the overall plan. If you're just starting a business, that is probably one of the first things you need to consider: getting leads. However, do not forget these leads have cost you money; they should be reflected in your budgeting and as part of overall costs. Whenever you produce a service or a product and sell it, make sure, as part of the overall costs, you also deduct how much the lead cost you, so you know the true net profit.

If you have never done any serious budgeting for your business, go back and analyse the historical financial statements for your business; they should give you an idea of how much budgeting you need for the coming year, plus any contingency aspects. Try to compartmentalise the budget. 'X' for marketing, 'Y' for advertising, 'Z' for materials, etc. You get the idea? Then, you will get the overall budget that you need, based on the activity of the years before, plus any future aspirations you have for your business. Budgeting has to be realistic and manageable; going over your budget constantly is like going into your bank overdraft constantly.

If, in the last year or two, you had good revenue coming in, or a lack of it, find out why this happened and how to do the same, or not do it, again. This also allows you to see how much more budget you need to dedicate to a certain aspect of the business after making reasonable assumptions about the future.

This is a summary of the financial aspects of your business in the recovery stage. Tailored measures for every particular business in your market have to be put in place in order to stand out. Some businesses are a twelve-month activity, while others are seasonal; some depend on the weather, and other on occasions, but the main principles are the same.

PART EIGHT

THE RECOVERY

DOING SOMETHING FOR THE FIRST TIME!

Have the courage to do something against the odds. When, in 1877, Henry Ossian Flipper became the first African-American graduate of an armed forces academy in the USA, he paved the way for others, who, out of love and duty for their country, wanted to serve in the in the armed forces, but maybe had their doubts whether they would be accepted or not.

Ret. Col. Clifford Worthy wrote in his autobiography, *The Black Knight: An African-American Family's Journey from West Point—A Life of Duty, Honor and Country*, how he, against all odds, made it as a cadet in West Point following a recommendation letter in 1946. The decision he made and the goal he set for himself shaped the rest of his life as a decorated US Army officer who later sat on a committee at General Motors.

His story, and the stories of men and women like Col. Worthy, tell us that if we want something badly, we have to make bold and against-the-odds decisions. This starts by having a dream, a goal, a plan and the guts to do it. If it happens, and usually it does happen, then you live the life of a victor; but, if it doesn't, then you have no regrets, as you gave it all you could.

Many people read and listen to thousands of great ideas and have plans, but never implement these ideas because of fear of failure, rejection, or what others might think.

Your business, your future and the lives of the ones around you need you to take bold and decisive actions.

Imagine letting yourself down, or all those loved ones who care about you and look up to you. I don't think one single book can deal with that kind of personal and moral recovery.

Be bold. In this book, there are many ideas and insights that you can adopt to make a difference. Start with goals, despite everything that goes around you; in your mind, block everything and plan your goals. Once your goals are clear, with a time frame in mind, plan how to get there. Start small, and give yourself and your team credit, then build up to bigger and more ambitious goals. You may surprise yourself with how capable you are; we all are in the face of adversity and crisis.

What is your business's legal and moral obligations in the pandemic?

At times, companies have to close completely or partially. Infected or suspect employees must stay at home. Employers have to make massive protection and organisational adjustments to meet new occupational safety requirements.

How does the virus Covid-19 affect employment relationships? What must a responsible employer do? What state support is out there?

CORONAVIRUS AND EMPLOYER DUTY OF CARE

Protection begins with comprehensive information about the risk of infection from the coronavirus and correct hygienic behaviour.

Within the scope of this general duty of care, when exercising their rights, the employer must take into account the wellbeing and legitimate interests of each employee, preventing the occurrence of damage to the employee, but also respecting their dignity and personality.

As an employer, you have had to...

Keep yourself up to date and pass on important current reports to employees.

Educate yourself about the development and symptoms of the infection.

Prohibit, cancel or postpone business trips, so employees do not feel obliged.

Encourage all employees to notify the employer if they have had contact with infected or suspected infected within the past fourteen days, or have been in an area at risk, contrary to warnings. Create a culture of transparency.

Encourage employees to wash their hands frequently, making it a lifelong habit.

Provide disinfectants in all facilities and office/workrooms.

Mouth and nose protection are recommended, and are required in exceptional cases (such as medical personnel in the infectious emergency room, etc..)

Prohibit physical contact with employees, e.g. no greeting by handshake.

Keep a minimum safe distance.

Sneeze and cough away and into the arm.

Instruct employees with symptoms, such as cough, fever or inability to breathe, to leave immediately and self-isolate or seek medical help, avoiding the company until cleared.

EMPLOYERS HAVE TO CREATE FRAMEWORK CONDITIONS

It is not enough to encourage employees to follow these hygiene rules. Employers must also create conditions for this in the work environment.

Workplaces may need to be redesigned in such a way that there is at least 1.5 metres between the individual workplaces, and, ideally, partition walls; in the case of workplaces with public traffic, the latter is now mandatory.

Disinfectants and other hygiene products must be provided by the employer.

Schedules for shifted working hours, breaks or times for changing clothes must be specified.

Special attention must be given to employees who belong to risk groups. People over the age of sixty and those with previous illnesses are considered particularly vulnerable groups of people in connection with the coronavirus. Accordingly, the employer who keeps their business open must pay particular attention to these employees.

The listed hygiene and handling rules are permissible as long as they are sensible and suitable and, in individual cases, the employee is not burdened unreasonably.

The general instruction for employees to wear a face mask or protective gloves, or to wash their hands on company premises, has to be clear and permitted.

The risk of infection in the workplace, not least because of the above-mentioned rules of conduct, should be kept as demonstrative and stringently low as possible, because the fear of possible infection—in addition to one's illness and the care of a sick relative—is one of the main reasons why employees could stay away from the company.

DUTY OF CARE AND LOYALTY: COHESION, MAINTAINING CONTACT AND DATA PROTECTION IN TIMES OF CORONA

Employees should be kept in constant contact with one another, regardless of whether they are infected, self-isolating or unaffected in their home office, and information should be exchanged. In this way, mutual ties are to be maintained and the resumption of operations, which needs to be carried out successively, is to be designed to run as quickly and smoothly as possible.

If authorities ask the company for information, for example, in connection with an infected employee, the employer must transmit the desired data.

THE CRISIS PARALYSES PUBLIC TRANSPORT: CAN WORKERS STAY AWAY FROM WORK?

The closure or restriction of public transport can make it harder for individual employees to come to work. This risk lies with the employee; they have to find other ways to get to their job on time. In times of car-sharing, electric scooters, driving services such as Uber, rental bikes, etc., this should be possible in most cases.

In case of an employee becoming infected because of their mode of transportation, there will be a need for investigating and tracing the source of the infection. Corresponding surveys must find out which other employees/people had direct contact with the person concerned. They are just as at risk as the infected person/person suspected of being infected and may need to be sent for the COVID-19 test.

As a direct consequence, the employer must take measures to protect all other employees. Continuing to work as before is no longer an option at this stage. In the worst case, the company is closed, and all employees are to be sent home until the danger has passed. This applies all the more to companies in which the risk of infection is particularly high, such as those who have prolonged contact with customers.

Paying extreme attention and instructing in personal hygiene is critical to avoid these problems for the business.

FUNCTIONING WHILE THE BUSINESS IS CLOSED

The burden on employers when a business closes and they are obliged to continue paying wages is extremely high, especially since it is completely uncertain how long this condition will last. Alternatives must, therefore, be explored, which can be considered depending on the type of company and the nature of the employment contracts.

HOME OFFICE IS THE BEST SOLUTION

The employer can have employees work from home if the nature of the work allows and their employment contract allows for this possibility.

COMPANY CLOSURES DO NOT MEAN FORCED COMPANY HOLIDAYS

Arranging unilateral holidays, for example, by deciding on company holidays, is not possible. When granting vacation, the wishes of the employee must always be taken into account. The pandemic situation does not fall under 'urgent operational requirements,' which would outweigh the interests of the employees in vacation determination. Mutual agreements are important in these cases.

REMOTE WORK OR TELEWORK

Working from home has, for some, started to become the norm during the lockdown, and has turned out to be quite manageable.

Some businesses with several branches throughout the country are now seeing the benefits of restructuring and reorganising in such a way that the workforce can do the same job from home with similar results as before, but without the extra costs of leasing and running office space.

This has become the work model that we had to assume during the lockdown, which means managing personal/professional life balance well and overcoming these five inconveniences:

1 | Say Goodbye to Social Life

The first annoyance is the most obvious; the loneliness that comes from confinement and working at home. Certainly, at the start, you may be happy that you no longer have to suffer the annoyance of a coworker in your office space, or the erratic personality of a colleague, but that also amounts to saying goodbye to your daily social life! The appointment at the coffee machine to start the day, the lunch breaks in the company canteen or on a terrace... Telework is a model that both sets you free and deprives you of relationships. Humans thrive on relationship, so this model can become challenging for some in the long run. Companies that decide to adopt this model even after the pandemic can arrange for not only routine virtual meetings, but also periodic face-to-face meetings to keep morale high and create a sense of belonging and community.

2 | Clothing Problem

Dress codes are like a shackle for many, and many teleworkers are happy to be able to give up suits or tailored clothes to work in casual attire. If, at the start, you enjoy sitting in your pajamas in front of your computer, you may quickly feel out of step with the image you have of a fulfilling, active life. Dressing, hair, make up for women, and so many other morning rituals certainly help one to take a professional posture and prepare psychologically for the challenges of the day ahead! Keeping up a professional appearance is good for some, if that gives them the extra motivation to act and behave a certain way. Some can even talk differently and have more confidence in themselves based on what they wear.

3 | Are You Really More Productive at Home?

The short answer is, not necessarily! Between cleaning, children, shopping and the desire for a good nap after lunch, it can soon become a nightmare to work from home. Beware of the trap into which many teleworkers fall, namely, to mix their personal constraints, or distractions, with professional commitments from a distance, the famous desire to kill two birds with one stone. The other trap generally comes from your loved ones, who feel that, as a teleworker, you are available enough at home to carry out additional tasks for the couple or the family (picking up the children from school, shopping, etc..). Teleworking requires a lot of discipline to maintain your productivity every day, while in the office, the question does not even arise!

4 | From Your Bed to the Computer, are You Finding Difficulty Separating Between Your Personal and Professional Life?

Some may find themselves in the same mood, taking on a relaxed, homey approach to work, which may work for some, but not for everyone. If you stop dressing professionally and do your household tasks at the same time as you are answering emails or making professional phone calls, you risk quickly and completely melting away the barrier between your personal and professional life. Getting out of bed and going directly to your computer, without going through the working-day 'wake up' routine, can cause your day to become less productive and professional. People will start noticing this, which cannot be good for the business.

5 | **Computer and Other Technology Failures**

Teleworking requires knowing how to manage on your own. No computer technician comes to the rescue if your computer or printer stops working, or when your Internet router refuses to function. No colleague can lend you an instant critical appraisal of a file that you manage or work on before you present it.

Remember, this is the time of coronavirus. In the event of a temporary lack of motivation, or a difficult or stressful moment, no one is by your side to help you decompress, except perhaps by telephone or email. Again, the absence of a social life may weigh on you, and, for some, become unbearable. Therefore, positive daily reinforcement and staying in touch with colleagues during working hours to exchange ideas may lessen some of the isolation that you feel.

TIPS FOR WORKING REMOTELY DURING AND AFTER THE PANDEMIC

❖ As much as possible, organize a professional space separate from your personal life, like a dedicated room or office.

❖ Make sure you have a good internet connection and communication tools with your employees (chat space, file sharing, etc..).

❖ Set fixed time slots entirely devoted to your work, as if you were in the office, and warn your loved ones that you will not be available, even if you are physically present at your home. Ideally, turn off any potential distractions.

❖ Replace what previously represented your preparation and transport time with an early moment for you, such as breakfast or going out for a walk, so as to not go directly from bed to your computer

❖ If you like to dress, do your hair or put make up on, go on and do it!

❖ If loneliness weighs you down, think about communicating with your friends using video chats and conferencing software or Apps.

In conclusion, revisiting the notion of teleworking, we notice that online meetings are becoming increasingly popular, especially in the current crisis climate, as web conferences have become the norm for many organisations.

Whether they are used for important appointments with customers, team meetings or conducting job interviews, web-based conferences offer a quick and practical solution.

However, running a web conference successfully is not something that all companies are familiar with, as some businesses have never done it before; they just found themselves in the middle of a crisis and had to use it because of the lockdown.

The advantages of web conferencing are many, particularly for company meetings; being able to do screen sharing or screen transmission is quite an innovative way of working in a group, as everyone can share their presentations and ideas online for everyone to see and collaborate on.

File sharing is not new, and some organisations have used it for years, but now they serve an important need, as employees no longer need to be present in the same place. It is safer for everyone, and they can still exchange files and important documents with ease, especially when a document has to be created or edited by many users. This way, they can all do it at the same time.

Having the ability to use a digital whiteboard for participants to collaborate, making notes or sketches to get their ideas across, can be a very valuable tool, at least for certain organisations.

In addition, participants seeing and hearing each other, and interacting with one another by using the chat boxes, is also proving to be another useful way of communicating in the post-pandemic era. This way, they can write down perhaps less urgent things for a meeting moderator to look at it and take care of the questions, directing them to the right people.

It's a very efficient way of working with a group, especially for a larger team.

Online video conferencing is slowly becoming part of most businesses, so perhaps you may want to try it to communicate with whomever you want to communicate with regarding your business. Perhaps it is time to look into some professional video conferencing solutions that will boost the image of your company. No doubt we will see many companies resurface and compete with each other again, and having an online presence like this can give your business an edge as another marketing tool to utilise.

One of the biggest advantages of these meetings is the ability to record. Obviously, everyone needs to be in know and must be told that it is being recorded, but the recordings could be archived for future use and training; in addition, they could be transcribed or used as meeting notes and memos, so that everybody can refer back to them when they want.

Online meetings can reduce the costs involved with expensive business trips, where employees used to spend countless hours in cars, trains and aeroplanes, staying in hotels and wasting days at a time. Now, they can conduct the meeting from the safety of their office or home. This, hopefully, will also reduce the company's carbon footprint, while keeping the meeting fully functional, and perhaps even more efficient than before, while contributing to saving the planet.

STRATEGIES FOR OFFICE REOPENING LAYOUTS AND RETURN TO WORK PROTOCOLS

As the pandemic is still looming in many parts of the world, companies are reopening their offices gradually, and one has to think about the fact that, at least for a while, we cannot be working in the same way we did before in these offices. New measures are taking place, especially since, at the current stage, there are no immunisation against the virus yet. To combat this situation, everyone is still depending on personal hygiene, contactless interaction with others, keeping enough distance from each other and, hopefully, general common sense.

It's heartwarming to see life going back to normal, to see businesses reopening and the economy slowly turning around and most services resumed. However, one has to think, if the current situation carries on for some time, how will workers function in a small office, and how will services be delivered in these tight offices?

Coming back to the idea of working from home and tele-work, which, on the surface, can be quite an efficient way to conduct certain aspects of business, how safe is the information that exchanges hands between employees' homes?

The majority of the western world's larger companies and banks outsource the majority of their customer calls. Most of the call centres are in a few countries because of lower labour costs, but when these people are not allowed to work in their offices and they have to work from home, dialing into the company to retrieve customer data, how safely guarded is this information, which involves customers' sensitive data?

There is a lot to be considered when outsourcing, but when the outsourcing companies send their people to work from home, that is another threat level that we need to be aware of.

With regards to office layouts, nowadays, they have to be such that it's safe for the employees to function efficiently, and for the customers as well. The problem is that most small businesses have small premises, which will probably not allow for that, as the only way to do this is by blocking off areas of the business so that it becomes safe to interact.

This obviously will have a huge implication on the speed of service delivery, efficiency and, more importantly, the level of revenue for the company.

There is no easy fix for this, and business owners have no choice but find innovative ways to deal with this problem. In fact, they are becoming more innovative every day in the way they deliver their services.

A lot of thought is needed to see how they can function in an office with limited space.

There is no doubt, as discussed before, that there will and should be price adjustments, as now businesses can only deal with half of the number of customers that they used to see during same time last year, yet are still expected to bring in the same level of revenue like the years before, because suppliers' invoices, utility invoices and other costs involved with running a business never stop.

In addition, there are the bank loans and other loans, and the charges that they have acquired during the first period of the lockdown.

Therefore, new ways of doing business will prove crucial for the survival of the business.

This could lead to a shift in products or services, or a shift in pricing structure. The way marketing and advertising were done before no longer apply; businesses now have to attract different demographics, possibly more affluent customers who don't mind paying extra for a great service or goods.

Business not as usual also means maybe changing the type of business that was provided before, such as a different product range, more of a particular product or service range, and multi-layered services.

If your business allows, try to have everything for your customers in one place, under one roof; this way, they get everything from your business, which is good for the business, while also doing your customers a favour by eliminating the need for your customers to go around and shop in various places. This is also safer for everyone.

This will probably be the model of the future, where we will find one type of business providing and selling various products and services all under one roof in order to maximise revenue and minimise customers' visits to other places.

Some of the larger companies have been doing this for decades, and now it is time for the small business to catch up. Everyone is in their niche, as small businesses, by nature, are more specialised, but that doesn't stop them expanding their range of products and services.

Looking at the office layout in some larger corporations, they have already introduced measures, such as employees securing a work-spot through an app on their smart phones that will assign them to a sanitised space from which they could work from throughout the day.

Floors and surfaces will be marked with arrows to clearly indicate directions. This has been seen more and more, even in communal spaces; however, when it back to a small enterprise, the question is how to deal with that practically. One of the ways this has been dealt with is by not allowing more than a certain number of people to enter the space, which means a slower rhythm of business and, of course, a slower turnover of business; this cannot be good for any business, or for the economy, in the long run.

These new norms have certainly changed people's behaviour; we notice now that, wherever we go, we look for the arrows on the floor in order to see the direction or the flow of traffic.

Other problems some companies are facing are their location, as some are located in high-rise buildings, where the only way to enter or exit the business is through lifts/elevators. Now that the amount of people will be restricted in each lift, how will this affect the traffic flow in and out of the business?

One solution could be to rent or hire other types of spaces with possibilities for better air circulation, such as low-floor and ground-level buildings where windows could be open, or working from leased spaces shared with other companies.

If no heavy technology and machinery is involved, this could be a solution model for some businesses, especially office-based businesses.

As a small business owner, you know best how your business functions and the frequency in which people come in and out of your business, but if, for whatever reason, you struggle with imaginative solutions, there are firms that can help you keep people safe coming in and out of your premises.

No doubt, there will be firms that specialise in this kind of problem solving; if you are stuck for ideas, one solution could be to go to one of these firms, explain your problem and see how they can help you.

In this day and age, where it's crucial to keep everything safe for health, safety and legal reasons, these firms may also provide you with legal documentation and certifications that could serve you later if, for whatever reason, a customer or one of your employees wanted to take action against you for not making the workspace safe enough.

Of course, this doesn't take the responsibility away from you; however, it will show that you've gone the extra mile to protect them and look after their wellbeing.

It is possible that someone can get ill or contract the virus from a shopping cart, or by touching a door handle, a product, or on any other number of occasions where we come in contact or touch something; however, while they are under your roof and in your business, employees are your responsibility, and they should not be asked to come back to work unless it's safe to do so and there are measures in place for them to be safe. All this has to be documented carefully, and, ideally, reviewed and signed by everyone to say that the environment is deemed to be safe and that they're happy to work in that environment based on the information that was available at the time.

Situations will be evolving all the time; therefore, you need to keep an eye out for the latest legislation regarding these topics, making sure you update your documents and policies regarding the workspace and making sure that everyone, including yourself, is safe to conduct business on the premises.

We have to rethink and reimagine new ways of work, and we have to change our old habits of doing things.

The entire history of humanity has been based around connecting and interacting with each other, but, all of a sudden, we are asking people to connect less, to not interact so much and keep their distance. This is not an easy ask, but if it means saving lives, then it seems like we have no choice.

In conclusion, providing a safe environment and a safe workspace for your employees is one of the first tasks that needs your total attention. Once that is done, only then can you ask people to come back to work.

PART NINE

STRATEGIES FOR SMARTER RECOVERY

MARKETING

I t is easy to get into the trap of thinking that, during the recovery period, there is no need to market your services or products because your customers are in lockdown and, once you reopen, they will be flocking back in.

On the flip side of that, what is enough and sufficient marketing that you need to do to attract your old customers back, plus potential new ones? Is there a magic number or formula or timing? Do we wait for a while, or start an aggressive marketing campaign? But, remember, everyone else is doing the same!

These are all questions that go through the mind of every business owner at this time, and there is no quick answer or fix to this issue, apart from one important thing:

Be visible! And be there for them when they come back!

Depending on your business and industry (online/offline business, or both), if your marketing budget has not been affected by the pandemic, then there is no harm in marketing intensely; just remember, as Dan Kennedy, the author of the No B.S. business book series, used to say, 'Fifty percent of marketing works and the other fifty percent doesn't, and I wish I knew which fifty percent is working!'"

If your marketing, among the other costs of your business, is on a shoe-string budget as a result of the pandemic, then making wise choices is critical, in order to not waste the time, energy and little money most businesses are left with under the current climate.

Becoming resourceful is a good idea in this situation. There are ample opportunities that may not cost a lot money, but have significant rewards, like staying in touch with your clients and welcoming them back to your business by means of calling them, sending emails and maybe even a short message on a postcard (which makes you stand out, as no one sends them any more), to remind them that they are on your mind.

Make sure you have incredible incentives for them when they return. This way, they feel looked after and appreciated. You do not necessarily have to drop your prices, but most businesses can add a lot of value to what they sell. Show them your appreciation for coming back to you and not going somewhere 'cheaper.'

For the so called 'brick-and-mortar' small business, it can be very hard to go online, let alone global; however, there are unique and innovative ways to make sure you spread your reputation and words beyond your local area.

One important recovery plan is to have a second, third and fourth business plan for the future. The key word is: diversify.

If your business has the chance to have an online presence, then do it, and do it properly. Think outside the box. Can you sell certain products or services online? Do it! Can you expand? Do it! Can you start another online business alongside yours? You guessed it: Do it!

Be creative with your thinking, your marketing and everything that touches your business. Think: Who are your target customers, plus who else do you want to come to you? Can you create other product lines or services to cater to other demographics?

You may want to have different tiers of products or services, or you may only sell to the affluent. It is a choice, and a decision you have to think about carefully.

Obviously, most business owners want to go back to where they left off before the pandemic and carry on as usual; however, this is a good time and an opportunity to reflect on where you want your business to be in five, ten, or twenty years, if you could have the choice. Despite the gloomy outlook of the economy, having a contingency plan or other options on how to conduct business can be the difference between surviving and thriving.

More than ever, your own personal brand, or that of your business, can play a huge role in recovery. You need to know that, despite all the hardship and personal sacrifices, you are still here, and even stronger, to be of service to them. Nothing beats how you market yourself. People may have wanted iPhones and iPads no matter what, but it was the late Steve Jobs' personality that became the magnet for people's loyalty and the rest is history. Do people buy Tesla because it is the only electric or sleek car? No! They buy it because of some unique features of course, but also because Elon Musk sprinkles on so much personality, which makes it so much more exciting to own his product.

The same goes for my co-author in my bestselling book, *Success 360*, Sir Richard Branson. Over the years, he made people feel as if they knew him personally, and that he is just another regular guy, though maybe with few extra billions and an island; that is the power of personal branding.

No matter what your business is, how large or small, do not forget the most important part of your company: YOU!

Brand and market yourself right, and people will come back to you, because they want YOU and your services. One of the masters of personal branding are barbers; people tend to drive miles to see 'their' barber or stylist. This isn't because they are the best in what they do, though maybe some are, but because of the human connection they create, possibly unknowingly. Imagine that on a larger scale. This is the time to show personality, and that you care about your customers on a human level, and not just for a transaction.

I think it is fair to say that we, as humans, learned a lot about ourselves and others during the pandemic, and that made some of us think twice about the way we conduct business. We just saw in front of our eyes how fragile can life be, and that everything can be taken away in a blink of an eye.

I hope people come together more after this, and that it only leads to more and better understanding, more respect for each other, and treating others like we want to be treated.

You are in business, selling a product or a service. Now, the economy is taking a downturn, and there is general hardship, especially among small to medium-sized businesses. Maybe this is the best time to show your personal brand and add some of that personal touch to your business, which was probably was lacking before.

Before spending tens of thousands on marketing, which is not bad if you know why and have the money, maybe it is time to review your personal brand and your company's identity, and see how that can become a success in the future, starting with customers and people with whom you lost touch.

Here is a list of examples of how personal branding can become a very powerful marketing tool:

❖ A friendly postcard or email, which resonates with you and your branding, may go a long way by just checking in on them and keeping in touch without selling them anything.

❖ Associate yourself 'under your new brand' with individuals and groups that may help your business, directly and indirectly, through social media groups and other associations.

❖ Pay attention to opportunities, as they may not always be obvious. A direct connection with someone may not lead to anything yet, but keeping the door open may lead to a much bigger opportunity through someone else they know. Never dismiss people or look at them as if they are no good to you or your business. You never know if the next big opportunity may come from an unexpected source. At the same time, be mindful of your time and resources.

❖ Try to have something unique to contribute, and stand out in the crowd by offering something people are unable to find elsewhere.

❖ It is not all about you: Make sure you understand other people's needs first, and find a way to help them. This will pay dividends in the future

❖ Be positive. Make it part of your brand; no one likes a pessimist.

❖ Make sure you develop a reputation of being an expert at what you do, and being a problem solver, through your services or products.

❖ Have a vision and share your vision. People admire someone with a vision.

❖ Be a role model. Do everything to the best of your ability, and then some. Be honest with yourself and others. Be someone others aspire to be like.

BUILDING STRATEGIC PARTNERSHIPS TO DOMINATE YOUR MARKET

Teaming up with other organisations can only make your own company more visible. Strategic partnerships with other companies, to complement their position and your position in the marketplace, is not something new; there are many large companies in this world, such as McDonald's, Mercedes-Benz, Pizza Hut, Coca-Cola and others, that have partnered with each other. There must be a great deal of truth in the fact that strategic partnerships can create influence and power in the marketplace.

Find other businesses that compliment your business and partner with them.

Partnership is not competition; partnership should have a compound effect.

They will be visible to your clients, and you will be visible to theirs. Whether you are in business of selling products or providing services, there are always benefits to having a strategic partnership with other businesses that have the same needs as yours and want to expand their market, just like you.

Now, imagine you multiply that by two or three or four times. How much of the market can you all have?

The notion of 'I'll just do it myself and I will be fine,' is a wrong way of thinking. Don't forget that some of these partners may have a better online presence than you could ever imagine tapping into, or one of these partners could have better access to a much larger client base that they stay in touch with through newsletters and calls. Imagine being visible to those tens of thousands of their clients, just because you decided to partner with them.

Now, imagine that against your 'I will just do it myself' attitude.

Which one, do you think, is more powerful and could benefit your business?

Don't overthink it or overcomplicate it. It's quite simple.

If you find a suitable enterprise to partner with, they are probably just as excited as you are about working together. This way, you have a good recipe for a successful partnership.

When you find companies to partner with, see if their style and work ethic resonates with yours; they could potentially be a great match, and there are great benefits to this sort of partnership. Just doing it by yourself will not achieve the customer numbers that partnership offers.

Imagine having 10,000 customers on your list, who may or may not come back for repeat business; now, imagine if you add to that two other partners, each with a modest 10,000 customers. Now, all of a sudden, you have access to 30,000 customers.

This may sound very simple, and partnership is nothing new; however, we all need to be reminded from time to time that, by strategic partnering, we are not giving a piece of our company away, but expanding our client base.

If you sell something once, you just had a sale.

If you sell multiple things to repeat customers, then you have a brand.

When people keep coming back to you to have the same service, or buy the same product time and time again, or try new services, then you have a brand.

Just remember one very important thing: If you go to someone to partner with, be prepared for the number one question they will ask you: What's in it for them? They might like you, and they may like your business, but they need to know what's in it for them and their business. The same goes for you when someone asks you to partner.

This has to be achieved with the least amount of involvement from their side, at least to begin with, as no one likes the extra work.

Just remember that, when someone says no to the partnership, it could be that they are just not ready right now, or they don't see it the way you see it. Never take it personally; just file that in your mental business folder and not your personal. They may even come back one day.

Some people might be cynical initially, while others may feel a partnership to be a time and resource waste for their company. Some business owners might be just happy to do what they do by themselves.

Try to respect their wishes; wish them good luck and move on to the next potential partner on the list.

You do not need hundreds of partners; in fact, most businesses can only manage only a few. The most important aspect is not having many partners, but that the partnership itself complements what you are doing and what they are doing. For example, if you are a law firm partnering with a tyre company, or partnering with a healthy juice company, that's the kind of partnership that, even from a customer's perspective, seems odd.

However, if you have a company dealing with household cleaning products, and you're partnering with a company that does domestic or commercial cleaning, and another who deals with only carpets, that's probably the perfect partnership, as you not in competition, and you all do different things while serving, more or less, the same type of clients.

When presenting to your potential partners, always make sure you have a plan, and always show them the problems you are all facing at the moment, such as the need for more clients or more services. Show them the passion that you have for this partnership, because remember, when they see that you have a plan for the partnership, and that you are solving problems with a great passion, most partners will be open to your suggestions, and they will be in a far better position to make a decision.

Just imagine, after the pandemic crisis, getting back to business but instead of dealing with your customer base, you also have access to many more clients because of strategic partnerships. How about that for a recovery plan?

Let us assume you only have 10,000 customers that may or may not want to come back straight away, at least in the first phase of recovery. Now, think if you have access to five times that. If 10 percent of your original 10,000 want to come back during the first six months, that's 1000, but if 10 percent of the 50,000 want to come and see you, that's 5000 clients.

What difference would that make to your bottom line? That's the power of partnership.

In the plan, make it all about the partnership and them, and not so much about you. Show them and demonstrate that you can accelerate their plans and the way you plan do that, and try to show how you will take away some of their problems and pain. That, for sure, will guarantee you a front seat in their mind.

Just be honest with yourself: Is this about you only, or is it about them and you collectively? When you present it to them, make sure it's about them, yet remind them that this is a partnership, and that you are not there just to improve their position, and that they have to do the same for you. It is a two-way street, as they say.

Preparation is the key, so be prepared when you go to meet your potential partners: read about them, make sure you know everything about them and make sure you're honest about your business as well. Present your business to them in a transparent manner. You need to present a solid case that shows how this partnership will enhance their bottom line and yours. Find out the problems of both companies and try to solve those problems. This will definitely impress them, because no one would like to sit down and spend valuable time listening to someone who is winging it; we can all smell that from distance.

Always be fully prepared, because when you are prepared, that's when your passion comes out at its best, and your chance of persuading others is much higher, because through preparation and commitment, you became more determined to get a 'yes' from them.

It is very difficult to expect a 'yes' when you are not prepared. When you are prepared, you impress yourself and you impress the ones around you, and that increases your chances to persuade and get your point across.

It is very difficult to justify to yourself and others when, deep inside, you feel like you are not who you say you are, or that you haven't done your homework. If that's the case, you cannot demand a 'yes' from them, because you yourself don't believe in what you are saying.

To initiate the first conversation with them, you may want to show initiative by helping them first and seeing how this partnership goes. You can always show appreciation by taking the first step to introduce them to your clients by mentioning their services, having their logo on some of your material or some other message to show your clients that you are in a partnership with a like-minded company that will serve their needs.

Once you do that, the other company will have to do the same for you. You can all start small, then slowly allow the partnership to grow until it becomes a marketing machine for both companies for years to come.

It is very importantly not to forget to listen to them by simply asking what it is they want to improve. Who knows? Maybe you have the key to solve one of their problems by just asking them simple questions about what they want. It could be more sales, for example, or it could be more clients, or less headache dealing with a certain thing. You may have the solution straight away to their problem, and you can help immediately.

Be honest and tell them why you want to work with them. Let them know that, after the pandemic crisis, everyone is nervous and needs more work, plus access to a wider audience and more visibility, without costing a lot more in marketing and advertising.

This is by far a better way to complement each other and help out each other, and it could become the fuel for other strategic partnerships. This way, you have security in your strategic partners, who are willing to help you as much as you are willing to help them, which can make everyone's position much stronger.

A strategic partnership is not all about joint ventures, or your clients getting their services and products in return for their clients getting yours.

Sometimes, partnering with an organisation that has access to certain skills, departments or business elements that you are lacking, can far outweigh a joint venture partnership. For example, if you have made a list of your strengths and weaknesses, and, out of your weaknesses, you find that there are a few things you've been working on for years but haven't improved much, such as efficiency, but you know this partnering organisation is known for being super-efficient and wasting no time, you can learn this from them, and your department can learn from their department. That's a life-long benefit for your company. Let's face it: Partnerships don't last forever; some last decades, and others don't. But, imagine if your organisation learned the best aspects of efficiency without wasting resources. How valuable do you think this will be to your organisation? Of course, you hope that you have something similar for them in return.

Think about what in your weakness list you can improve on by partnering with others, and what's in your strengths list that you can bring to the table. You must have some strengths; otherwise, you wouldn't be in business all these years.

Present your arguments and help them out, because that's the true meaning of a partnership. If that happens, everything else will follow, but that only happens if you are true to yourself and if you know exactly where you stand in terms of strengths and weaknesses.

So, if you're wondering how to partner with someone, or with whom you should form a strategic partnership, you can simply make a list of your company's strengths and weaknesses. It is very important to be honest with yourself when making the list. From there, you can look at your weaknesses and ask yourself what other companies around you are doing that better than you are. Maybe you can approach them for partnership.

Just be warned that they may not see it the way you see it. Try to be totally prepared, because when you are fully prepared, even if they say no to the partnership, they will respect you for taking the time to prepare, and they will keep you in mind. Who knows? Maybe today they say no, but tomorrow, they will come back and ask for your partnership, or another type of collaboration.

Remember to always ask yourself: How can you be of service to them, and what can you do to improve something they are not as good as you are? That is what may potentially open the door in to their world.

What is in it for them?

You can always begin your conversation with them by saying that you have learned a lot about their organisation by doing research, mentioning that you are very impressed, but it seems to you that they may like to do more of this or that, and if that's the case, you want to present some ideas as to how they could get more of what they want by borrowing from your strengths in that department.

By just asking if they are interested in hearing these ideas, you make it sound like you are just having a normal conversation. Be genuine at all times.

Strategic partnerships are all about give and take. You have to dig deep to see exactly what you need, and be very specific; in return, find what they need, and try to establish a connection that way.

Once you do your due diligence about the connection between your company and their company, ask them if they agree that that's the case. Ask if you are missing anything, and let them open up to you and tell you what other things are missing. That's where you can search within your own capabilities and strengths to try to genuinely help them. Consider this: As a small-medium business owner, you are not partnering with a conglomerate; you are partnering with like-minded companies that also have strengths and weaknesses. No one company can be all about strengths or all about weaknesses, because if they think they are all about strengths, they wouldn't even entertain the idea of talking to you; in contrast, if they're all about weaknesses, well, then, they probably won't still be in business by the time you finish this book!

Think about this idea of strategic partnership and imagine this strategic partnership happening with the organisations you most admire in your industry that serves the same demographics. Just imagine what would that do for your business.

If you think it will do good for you and your business, then prepare to the maximum and knock on their door to present your case.

If, however, at this moment, you don't feel right, or you don't have the right 'gut feeling' about them, then perhaps it's time, just for now, not to do that partnership, because you need to feel good about what you are doing; otherwise, it will all sound fake, and you will come across as ingenuous, and that may destroy any deals you could ever make with them.

So, make your list, choose your partners, learn all about them, plan what to present to them, knock on their door and present your case—and, who knows? With your dedication and passion and wisdom, by next year, you will be looking back, thinking perhaps that was the one of the most important things you have done this year to improve the situation in your company, not only as part of a post-pandemic recovery plan, but also as a move that will prove useful for years to come. You can build other partnership alliances on the back of this, and who knows where would that lead to, so be positive, be the leader you know you are, take the reins and start looking for partners.

REPUTATION MANAGEMENT THROUGH CUSTOMER EXPERIENCE

We all know how important customer experience is and how vital it is for your business. Now, more than any time before, an excellent customer experience is crucial for your business, as businesses will be competing for customers and you need to stand out, and fast!

Everyone is familiar with the phrase 'customer satisfaction is vital,' but what needs to be added is 'customer loyalty is far more important.' It is the bottom line of any business, and therefore, in this post-pandemic era, you need to make sure that your customers' experience is such that they become loyal to you and not just satisfied, as my good friend, Howard Partridge, is always advocating in his programmes.

Howard is an amazing human being. As the president of Phenomenal Products Inc., he helps small business owners transform their businesses through systematising the business, among many other things. He came up with a term that sums it all up: exponential marketing. In his book, *The Five Secrets of a Phenomenal Business*, Howard describes exponential marketing in great detail. For this unique marketing message to happen, we need to look at five points. Here is my brief take on those five points:

1 | **Reputation:** Your old customers are loyal customers already; they know you and they know your reputation, and perhaps they were part of establishing and anchoring this reputation. However, like any other business , new customers and clients need to trust you before they can do business with you. So, use everything you can to establish that reputation with them.

In addition to providing a top-notch service consistently and persistently, I have found that one of the most effective ways to do this is to look at companies with great reputations and analyse them, seeing why they have that reputation. What are they doing differently? Is it because of their product? Is it because of their service? Is it their branding, or the way they position themselves, or all of the above?

There are a lot of clues around. You can look at your own business and see where you can add value. You can also work on your branding and how to make the experience unique for your customers, which will potentially create an excellent reputation for being the best in your market.

One important thing you can do is, to educate your clients, taking them on a discovery journey about the process of doing things in your company. If you have an amazing product, you can explain how the product is made, the quality of the product and how this quality is measured, plus many more things that you can come up with for your own industry and niche.

This is a good way of establishing a good reputation.

Unfortunately, reputation doesn't happen overnight, and reputation doesn't happen because of one single product or service; it's a multitude of things happening together, with your permission and under your control.

It is a combination of the quality of the product, the quality of service and, very importantly, the quality of delivery and follow up, and how professionally it's all been delivered.

All these things together will give you a reputation that your competitors might not necessarily have.

Marketing your reputation is done by using what others say about you, rather than what you say about yourself. This is why businesses use genuine testimonials and endorsements. That's all part of reputation management, demonstrating trust and proving that you have an excellent reputation.

2 | **Experience:** By this, we mean your experience. Customers ask whether you have the experience to do what you say you are doing. They might trust you as a person, and they might trust the business, but they're not sure how much experience you have, so, in your marketing message, you have to show and prove that you are experienced.

There many phrases that people in business use to describe their experienc;, some of the most common ones we see are things like, 'since 1985 doing XYZ,' or 'we have over twenty-five years of experience.'

These statements, and many more, can be used to show your experience. We have seen a lot of these on product brands; they put how long they've been in business, and that creates trust, guaranteed.

If you haven't been in business for very long, you can focus on areas of experience that you have. You can market yourself with education and certifications, or if you're licensed to do certain things. Compared to others, who might not be certified or licensed like you, that is your competitive edge.

Any specialised training you or your staff have gone through that will benefit the customers needs to be mentioned to market your experience.

3 | **Education:** It's important to show in your marketing message your educational background and certifications to do certain things, as it will cement your reputation in people's minds.

4 | **Systems:** This is about your services and delivery systems, and how you will save the customer a headache and money in your specific way better than the competitor, and what makes you stand out from the competition.

For all this to happen effectively, you have to have systems that show your client and customer that you are different, and why they should come to see you or come back if they haven't been for a while.

If your business provides a service in a unique way that makes the customer very happy, but you have no system to talk about it and communicate it with others, then you are missing a great opportunity.

You can win many clients over by tapping into the emotional distress they have with another business. It could be they don't like the product, service or delivery; try to identify your competitors' shortfalls and deliver it to the customers, and see what happens next. They will think of you as a hero, saving them the headache of going to a substandard company, who probably have the same products, but don't have a system like yours to deliver it. Find out what it is they don't like about your competitor, then try to serve your customers better by promising to fill the gap, explaining what you do and why you do it that way. It shows you care about their needs. This how important systems are.

5 | **Guarantee:** Usually, small businesses are reluctant to offer guarantees on their products or services, but, at the same time, when a customer is not happy, they will very happily and promptly rectify the situation in order to keep the customer satisfied (and hopefully loyal). This is one way of trying to manage the company's reputation.

So, the big question here is: If you are so good at looking after your customers in such an honest and amazing way, and your products and services are top quality, why you don't shout about it in your marketing?

Tell the world how you do business and how you look after your customers.

But, you may ask, what about people who want to take advantage of the guarantee system? Well, you will always have people like that in life, and you just have to bear that in mind and factor that into the cost of doing business. One way or another, some people will always want to return their products, or they will decline services and want their money back. Of course, you still have to honour that because of your principles .

In that case, why not make a marketing statement and invite more people in to do business with you based on quality services and your guarantees?

Percentage-wise, you will still be better off, even if you have to give a refund to a few out of many.

This is still more profitable than giving no refund to zero customers, if that makes sense.

It is the same as 'ten percent of something is better than hundred percent of nothing!'

Your guarantee should be as strong as possible; this is obviously very different from product or product, or from market to market, but the more guarantee you offer, the more likely people will get your product or service, and the more they will trust you. It's common knowledge that no one offers a guarantee if they're not sure of the service or product they are offering.

So, it is a win-win situation; it gives the customer peace of mind and creates trust at the same time.

Your guarantee should be as strong as you are! It gives you a marketing edge, and more customers will be willing to do business with you.

Don't forget that your guarantee can be revisited and updated often; that way, you can see how it works for you. If it doesn't, you need to find out why, because if you have too many returns, that's not an indication that too many people are trying to take advantage of you, but perhaps that there is a problem with your product or service that needs to be addressed quickly. Before your competitor finds out and addresses the issue, you might want to address it yourself before it is too late.

PART TEN

THE SEVEN SYSTEMS YOUR BUSINESS SHOULD NOT BE WITHOUT!

When we say 'business NOT as usual,' we mean this in two ways: First, business is not as usual in the global sense as a result of the pandemic crisis and lockdown, and the economic aftermath. That is, the business of running everything in this world is not as usual anymore. The norms have changed.

The second meaning is personalised to you and affects you and your business. Your business not as usual in the sense that you cannot run your business as you used to run it before, and you need to pay attention to certain elements and aspects of your 'new ways' of running your business.

In the bestseller, *The E-Myth: Why Most Small Businesses Don't Work and What to Do About It*, Michael Gerber describes the necessity to systemise your business, which can be called the business development process. He goes on by saying if you do not systemise your business, the outcomes can be tragic!

According to Gerber, systemising a business can be done by any small-medium business owner and doesn't require an army of consultants, which is good news for any business owner. If it is done properly, the process could be used as a blueprint or a turnkey for other ventures and businesses to follow.

Almost everyone on Planet Earth probably knows about McDonald's, the fast food restaurant chain. The only reason they exist today, and became such a symbol for success, was because of their systems.

They are one of the masters of systematisation, masters of the business development process, as everything is systemised to the finest detail, from the moment you walk in or sit in your car in the drive-thru until you get your order.

Most small business owners know this and have seen it, and they know how prudent this is for their business to have some sort of system, and yet they don't!

They might have techniques for doing certain things in certain ways, or habits, but that doesn't qualify as a business development process.

When you have a system in place, then your service and product delivery can be faster, more efficient, consistent and perhaps cost less to produce, which ultimately leads to more profits. Most small business owners are aware of all this, but somehow, they don't act on it.

What stops them? Is it because they think that their business is different?

The answer is, yes. For some, it is the usual excuses, that that model of business is not their business, or the model doesn't apply to them, or they cannot see any benefit in doing so, or simply they just don't know how to do it.

So, they are stuck!

When a fifty-two-year-old salesman of milkshake machines, Ray Kroc, saw how a simple hamburger stand operated, he immediately recognised the huge potential the humble hamburger stand and the two brothers who owned it had, and what a gold mine they were sitting on.

Ultimately, he persuaded the McDonald brothers to let him recreate the franchise model.

Now, I'm not saying that your business will be McDonald's, nor that we should compare it to McDonald's, or even that you want to be McDonald's (to each their own), but we are talking about a foolproof business model based on systems that can produce consistent results time and time again.

The McDonald brothers were efficient; they created the original system and were happy to keep operations small, which, by the way, is a fine model, but Ray Kroc took it to a whole different level by adding other layers of systems until it became one of the most successful business models in the world.

A system is usually defined as the various parts of a business doing various things in certain ways and sequences, producing certain things at certain times, all predetermined and programmed, and everything working together in harmony.

You may need to read that again!

Looking at your business, you will know what the important steps are, from a client calling or visiting your business, making an inquiry, showing interest or purchasing something, and how you follow it up afterwards, after the service or goods transaction has taken place.

On the surface of it, that is not so difficult, or is it?

After all, it is what you do day in day out. The question is, can you repeat it in the same way, delivering the same results, by applying the same amount of effort and resources, without any fluctuation?

Also, can you scale it so that others can do the same at the same level of efficiency?

There are numerous resource materials out there, courses, manuals and gurus, who all talk about systems.

So, finding information on how to systemise your business should not be difficult, yet many still don't do it.

Some might feel that a system could create a trap; they think it will stop their creativity, since they have to follow a certain routine, but they can be wrong, because a system creates control over aspects of your business that would lead to better results more efficiently, ultimately creating less headache and more time for you to spend doing other things.

One main ingredient of any system is accountability in doing the things you say you are doing in the sequence you want to do them by making sure there is a quality control in place to see the system being implemented properly and correctly.

One could argue that, in a system, if one part isn't working properly, the whole system may collapse, or at least stop temporarily, and although there might be some truth to that, you can always build corrective measures in the system and contingency plans for every step in the system, so that when something doesn't function the way it should, the contingency plan or the corrective measure will start and rectify the situation.

Systems are used everywhere, especially in larger companies, which depend on systems to function. So, what stops the small-medium enterprises from having a very solid system in place?

It is understandable that this might be outside the comfort zone of many business owners, going back to basics and trying to create a business plan or model for the business that they have operated for years; however, this should be considered as an update, an upgraded version of their business, an improved version.

Creating a system for every department in your business is the key to making everything work smoothly together on top of the primary objectives, which is what you want to achieve out of your business.

You should have a system for your marketing strategies, management strategies, organisational strategies and, of course, your 'people' strategy and the delivery of services or products. Each element of these can have a system of its own, where they can all integrate together into one big system that makes everything work in harmony.

Having a system means clarity, and clarity equals better business. Here are the seven most common business systems used in a small business:

1. A financial management system that controls the flow of capital, which includes transactions, accounting and financial data for analysis and review. As most decisions in a business need financial backup, understanding your finances is crucial for a successful operation.

2. An employee management system that acts as your HR department and deals with everything that has to do with employees, which is what, in today's crisis, most businesses have been concentrating on: how to manage staff, manage expectations and keep them safe.

3. A customer development system that manages customers' needs and their journey from the beginning to the end, how to keep them, what kind of experience they had and, at the same time, how to look after new prospects and leads, from their first contact with the company through to providing the service.

4. An operations management system, which deals with customer value involving product services, quality management of responses and feedback, and economic value.

5. An improvement management system that deals with performance and how to improve it, customer feedback and contingency plans.

6. An equipment management system, which deals with how the equipment and tools necessary to deliver the service are functioning, being maintained and what can be done in case of failure. It deals with the various maintenance plans and intervals, and, in case the information management system fails and causes technology failure, what needs to be done to operate again as quickly as possible.

7. A company management system (which could be number one on the list), which deals with the company's strategy, aims and objectives, the monitoring of the company's performance, and how management at different levels are working together.

Creating systems or systematising your company can be easier than you might think, as most of the things that you do, perhaps automatically and instinctively, are part of your habits and the culture of your business, or 'the way you do things.' The only difference is that when you turn it into a system, it will save time and allow your business to grow, and you can avoid issues and problems that may be the result of the inefficiency of simply not having a system in place. Systems improve productivity and certainly lead to your business thriving even more .

In order to create systems for your business, you need to look at the repeated tasks and operations that keep happening all the time and affect your business, both in a good and bad ways.

It is probably easier to identify the issues that frustrate you the most, because, in your mind, they are on top of your list, simply because they irritate you all the time, such as things that you ask employees to do but they forget to do it, or don't do it the way you want. A hit-and-miss operation is never good for business.

This is one area of your business that perhaps requires the most urgent system creation.

System creation is not just about what needs doing, but how it needs to be done, from how you measure operations to how to follow-up on every aspect of the operation.

Some businesses have good systems for marketing, and they do it successfully, yet after going through all the trouble of marketing and advertising, they don't have a system for what to do with the prospect once they raise their hand and show interest.

We are surrounded by systems, and it is worth observing others: what they do right and what they do wrong. However, keep in mind the fact that you are perhaps only observing what is 'on stage,' and the reality is that there are many other moving parts behind this that we cannot see, and they're all working together backstage in order to make everything run smoothly.

So, until you do it and find out for yourself, you cannot imitate someone else's system fully. You can get ideas, and be inspired, but it has to be yours.

So, sit down and look at your business split into departments, create your vision and objectives, and see what you want to ultimately achieve out of your business and out of these systems. Then, try to imagine and write down all the activities that happened in each department in the past. Look at each department separately and see what frustrates you the most, and what you would change if you could just wave a magic wand. Now, you will come up with solutions, and it's these solutions that are combined together into a step-by-step system.

Have your own magic wand and create what you want. After all, it is your business!

Despite business not being as usual globally, be proud that your business 'will NOT and should NOT' be as usual from now on! It will be better, because now you are thinking with focus, you are planning and implementing more, and you are creating systems; this is how you make your business successful in the face of temporary hardship.

This is your time to shine. This is your time to change your business by making sure it's better than what it was before, that it achieves and serves the purposes that you outlined for your business.

Rest assured that the more focused you are on these aspects of your business, and the more you dedicate your time and energy to everything, the higher the rewards will be: having more free time, more satisfaction, feeling much better about yourself and, of course, having a much more successful and thriving business.

Never forget: You hold the magic wand!

PART ELEVEN

DON'T COPY APPLE!
THERE IS BEAUTY IN BEING SMALL!

While it's very inspiring to study companies like Apple, Amazon and others, and listen to their CEOs and founders giving encouraging messages, the truth is that, as a small-medium enterprise, you do not have the scope or the infrastructure these large conglomerates have.

Some might say that 'business is business,' and while there is truth in that, the reality is that these large companies can take hits during economic downturns and still survive (at least for some time), unlike the small-medium business, because they can afford it.

They can lower their prices, they can increase production and they can find new supply channels.

We have all seen how airline companies and other companies have advertised their products cheaply in the past whenever they wanted to increase sales, but, for the small business, this may not be sustainable in the long run. It works for them better than it works for a small business for obvious reasons.

The best way for a small-medium business to study other businesses and learn from them is to study and observe other successful small-medium businesses, ideally those in the same niche market, if possible.

Many times, you may find yourself in conferences or listening to educational materials for another type of market, yet it still makes sense for your market because the size of the businesses is similar, and it deals with similar levels of customer base.

Most entrepreneurs enjoy reading about Steve Jobs, Bill Gates, Jeff Bezos or Jack Ma, and while very inspiring and uplifting, their businesses are different to yours, and not everything, in fact, most of what they say doesn't apply to a small business.

So, watch out comparing a small, ten-employee business (and, by the way, there is nothing wrong with that) to a 20,000-employee business. They exist in two different business worlds.

Regardless of your business size, be proud of your business. Be proud of what you created. Be proud of the service and products you are helping people with. Be proud of the fact that, out of all the other businesses, small and large, people come to see YOU.

It could be for the uniqueness of your service, or your personality; most loyal customers will never exchange that for anything.

Not always, but some small businesses have a 'bigger version,' of thousands of employees who probably deliver the same product as yours, and perhaps even more efficiently than your small business. Yet, people still come to see you, rather than going to them, because they know that you look after your reputation with everything you can, and that you will deliver, and if, for whatever reason, they are not happy, you will try to fix it straight away, rather than having them go through hoops and ten phone calls and emails while they're still not getting anywhere. That means a lot to many.

Have you ever thought about that as a unique marketing positioning for your business?

Have you ever said in your advertising: 'Dear customer, you are one call away from getting what you want without any hassle?' If not, then think about it.

In this day and age, you can book any flight, or any hotel you like, with a few clicks on your computer through one of the big conglomerate online travel agents, and yet, some of the small-business travel agencies on the high streets are still operating and thriving.

Why do you think that is?

People like a personal touch. People like to know that they can speak to the same person again and that if they have any question regarding their travel arrangements, they can just pick up the phone and talk to someone they know, rather than talking to someone in a distant country who's been outsourced by another company and has no clue who you are and what your specific needs are—and heaven forbid if your plans changed and you wanted a refund!

There is beauty in being small, and there's beauty in appealing to loyal customers. Not every large business has made it over the years. In the post-pandemic economy, we will probably see an interesting shift in people's purchasing behaviour. There's an argument for small businesses to be successful again, and even thrive in this economy, if they choose to stand up back on their feet and if they know what to change and how to change it.

This gives reassurances to the consumer, and perhaps they would much rather deal with companies that deliver what they promise and guard their reputation.

We have all had our fair share of misfortunes with larger companies, who either disappeared because their profits dropped a bit, or their business model was not sustainable.

Larger companies in the travel industry and some airliners have been refusing to refund people during the pandemic; instead, they have been issuing vouchers. This has angered many customers, who will be looking for alternative companies to give their business to in the future.

People's behaviour and psychology has changed, and the way the economy is heading guarantees more change in people's purchasing behaviour.

This is your time to shine as a small business, and you need to be able to tap into these behavioural changes by starting to talk more about your business and marketing it in alignment with the new psychology.

Successful businesses solve people's problems. Very simple!

Just look at Amazon, for example. Is it the cheapest for purchasing products?

Probably not. But, are they one of the most efficient companies when it comes to delivery?

Yes. During the pandemic, many more people flocked to Amazon to buy goods, both necessary and unnecessary, and they went to Amazon because of one main reason: delivery. People knew the goods would be delivered on time, and that's what mattered to them, knowing that they would get what they ordered, and soon.

This just shows that price is important, but not everything.

Therefore, as a small business, unlike the large businesses, try not to get into a price war or price advertising, as that will be one of the worst things you could do when you still have to deliver a lot of value.

You try to generate a lot of good value by delivering a great, timely service, maybe with guarantees, so why destroy all that by advertising a cheap price? It doesn't make any sense!

People who did business with you in the past will definitely come back to see you again, because they are happy to do business with you for your integrity, honesty, delivery and quality of service, and nothing can beat that, so there's no need to advertise your cheapness when you know you deliver all that to your customers.

The reason people have been coming back to you, year after year, is simply because they like something about you, or they like something about your business, and they will make sure to go out of the way to come and do business with you.

Occasionally, you may need to remind them by sending a postcard or an email, maybe with an incentive, such as a little gift, anything that your imagination and budget allows you to do.

You just need to do the right things and the right steps in the right order; but whatever you do, do not get into the trap of a price war.

Country to what some might think, today's small business can and should charge higher prices for the benefits that the small business can offer compared to a larger business.

You have to make sure that your positioning is right to attract the right type of people, who appreciate your business and are willing to pay a higher price because, ultimately, they will get a better service and value for their money, through customised and tailored service for their specific needs.

Therefore, do yourself a favour and do not price advertise, especially cheap prices, as that will only attract price shoppers, and price shoppers will keep your business busy for no good reason. You will be busy looking after people who don't appreciate you, but your cheap prices.

During the recovery phase, every business is looking at how to stay afloat, how to go back to their success levels as before, and every business will be looking at customer traffic through their business and how to deliver efficiently.

These issues, plus many more factors, can play a significant role in how speedy the recovery will be for your business.

One aspect that almost everyone is thinking about is whether or not to raise prices.

There is an understanding that prices will have to go up after economic hardship, so that businesses can recover fast, but what if customers don't want to pay?

Perhaps that depends on the industry and the market. In certain industries, if they all raise their prices, one has no choice but paying the new price.

Most people know that, at some point, prices will go up, because businesses have to make up for the losses they had to endure during the crisis.

Sometimes, business owners overthink these matters and worry about things that may or may not happen, such as their worry about a small percentage price increase.

As a business owner, you know your products and services more than anyone else, and the value in what you are producing.

I encourage you to sit down and look at your pricing. Maybe this is a good time to play around with some figures, such as increasing a percentage on some of your products while keeping other products in the same price range. If something is more difficult to find, or it takes more time to do, then maybe you can increase it by a certain percentage. However, all this has to happen in an ethical manner, and without taking advantage of the fact that just because there's a shortage for a particular product, or there's too much demand (such as face masks and hand sanitizers, for example), that their prices should shoot up by 500 percent, which might be good for the business in the very short term, but it can also be very damaging in the long run. It will certainly affect your reputation and trustworthiness, as you cannot look people in the eye and tell them that you treat them with respect and dignity while you take advantage of them.

Consequently, since you are not taking advantage, for certain products, you can add a small percentage, just to make up for the initial lack of customer traffic; then, you can review it again once business is back on track, and if the figures indicate that your business is on a good recovery trajectory, you can decide whether you will carry on with that price structure or not.

As you run a small-medium business, people will understand that you had to include a small percentage increase in order for the business to continue and serve them in the best possible way in the future. If you are not around anymore, they may have to go to your competitor, who probably will not look after them the same way.

Remember, you are in business because you care: You care to do something meaningful for yourself, your family and others; you care and you're proud of delivering products and services to help people. You are a problem solver to your customers, so remember that, because you care, when you add a percentage, and when you find the right formula that works for your business, always see what else you can add, in order to add value and keep your customer feeling happy and valued. These could be things that don't cost the business much, or maybe nothing at all, such as lifetime support, or consultation for that product. These might be things you're already doing, because you care and that's your nature, but people don't even know about.

Customers might not remember or be familiar with that extra guarantee offer, or with the extra consultations and advice you give. They need to be reminded of these things as added value, because, most of the time, they see the product and the service and the pricing, and they compare it to other things, and usually that's where it ends, because that's how the majority of people are doing business.

But, you are not the majority of people; you are different, and you need to shout about it and market it, making sure you remind them gently and often why they are doing business with you.

There is a huge level of satisfaction in knowing that you don't just have the plans for a successful recovery, but also are planning to make your business thrive and making it future disaster-proof.

You may need to read certain parts of this book more than once and revisit some of the points that have been discussed, as information in general can be overwhelming when it's all delivered in one chunk. That's why we always encourage you to focus on the most important elements that will bring your business back on its feet, to create momentum and make sure you don't lose it, because it's that momentum that will help you in your uphill journey to take your business to new heights and become very successful.

The world of business is full of great advice from excellent business consultants, coaches, books and programmes. However, for the time being, and while your business is in recovery mode, try to concentrate on the few things that matter the most for your business recovery so that you do them very well.

This is why this book, and the information this book is providing, is written with this in mind, so that you can pick a chapter, full of advice, steps and tool kits, to implement immediately. It's written in a way that everyone can relate to, one way or another.

Therefore, as we said in the beginning of the chapter, as inspiring and encouraging it may sound studying other large businesses, maybe your time will be better used studying ideas that relate directly to the nature and size of your business, rather than large conglomerates who cannot be compared to small and medium-sized businesses at all.

Hopefully, one day soon, everything will be the way we want; then, you will have ample time to look into anything you want, but, right now, your business needs you and needs your focus.

In this book, we briefly talk about creating systems, which is very crucial, as it allows you to know and understand your business model and your customers better. Once this has been mastered, it can open doors to other opportunities regarding other businesses, partnerships or even expanding your current business.

This crisis made everyone reflect more, and look deeper into themselves and their businesses. We want to make sure the recovery journey is not just a survival journey, but rather a successful and thriving one.

THE BEGINNING OF THE FUTURE

This could well be the beginning of the future 'you' as a leader, or the future of your business as a company with a unique mission and vision, with exceptional services and products.

If you read this book, something tells me you are striving to be the best, and the only way we can have the best version of ourselves or our company is by changing things for the better. It all starts with your new vision and goal setting, and the ability to implement them.

Today is the pandemic; tomorrow could be negative economic growth as a result. Later, we may face another unthinkable problem. The key here is to be ready for bouncing back and taking a positive view, as with every downturn, there is usually an opportunity to grow and change things.

In this section, we will go over some of the recovery plan aspects already discussed as a reminder, and also go over some new ways for conducting business and perhaps allowing ourselves to be taken out of our comfort zone initially in order to not just survive, but thrive as a leader and in business.

No one can promise a fast recovery, but recovering fast is achievable and possible; it just depends on the willingness and level of implementing your plans.

Normally, in 'happier' times, businesses change one or two things at a time for an incremental transformation, analysing the response and outcome before moving to the next phase of change. However, if we are aiming for a fast recovery, many changes need to happen together, as time is of the essence here to bring the business back on track.

PART TWELVE

THE TOP TEN STRATEGIES FOR A SUCCESSFUL RECOVERY

As pandemics don't come around very often (thankfully), many businesses have no contingency plans for how to deal with them. Here are my top ten strategies for a successful recovery:

1. **Risk Identification:** Certain companies are IT heavy, others have products on shelves, some are just service-oriented with no products on shelves and limited IT needs and so on. However, they all must share one thing, namely, a disaster plan. Downplaying the risks can only lead to a problem later when disaster strikes.

   Therefore, during the recovery phase, the first thing to do is make sure that the company's infrastructure is ready for the recovery business, even though it might be at a slower level. This is important for the survival of the business. How technology and human resources are used efficiently, and dealing with suppliers and customers who have been on hold for a while, are all important aspects of the recovery phase, and require providing staff with adequate technology if they can work remotely, or if not, then making the environment safe for them. Both management and staff need to be re-educated in the new ways things work.

A pandemic planning and management task force or department is required for larger enterprises to oversee new policies and make sure that corporate governance is adhered to for a smooth-functioning enterprise during and after the pandemic.

Once a recovery business continuity plan is drawn, regular testing is essential for making sure that everyone knows their roles without any risks to themselves or the business. If a test fails, then it needs to be readdressed and the plan adjusted so that it passes a new test. Small businesses are known for lacking systems, and if one part of the system fails, especially during hard times, the rest of the system will suffer damaging consequences for the business.

2. **Be an Inspirational Leader:** Great leadership is needed now more than ever, and you have to show it if you take your business seriously. Your team and employees are looking for answers and reassurances, not just during the pandemic, but after as well. While you may not know more than anyone else, people still expect you to have answers; therefore, being current with crisis knowledge and taking an interest in what goes on in the world around you, and specifically in your industry, can and will make a big difference as you develop your pandemic communication strategy in the company. More than ever, you need your team to be fully behind you, and if they do not believe in your leadership, then they may not stand behind you or the business. A great leader is a knowledgeable leader, a resourceful one, and someone who cares about others

deeply. Respect is earned, and when people see you are there for them and do everything you can to protect them and their families, respect is natural. In the section 'How People Behave During a Oandemic Crisis,' we summarised the different personality traits and how people may behave differently to the same problem, and how you, as a leader, have the ability to show sympathy and understanding, gaining their trust while easing their anxiety.

A contingency plan, and part of making people feel valuable, is cross-training in different roles, so that employees can be active and step into new roles when needed.

3. **Have a Goal**: This is your business that needs to recover and hopefully thrive soon, so taking the time and setting your goals can only give you more clarity as to where you are heading. We may not have much control over the world around us, or what governments are doing on our behalf and how they may help or not, but at least in this aspect of the business, we have total control. Even if some of those goals are delayed and not implemented straight away for strategic or financial purposes, nevertheless, they are all written down, and you can go back and revisit them later.

4. **Get to Know Your Business More**: Some business owners have only a vague idea how their businesses function. That may not be you, but there are some out there who just show up on Monday and, just because they have a good product or service (possibly done by other team members), they just tick along, week after week, without seeing or understanding the big picture. Now is the time to understand your business' big picture. In the financial section of this book, we discussed in some detail how to be on top of the financial aspects of your

business. Do whatever it takes! If it means hiring people to teach you, or learning new financial skills, like understanding spreadsheets, reading or analysing financial charts, predictions or learning about other financial aspects of your company, this is the time to do so.

5. **Get to Know Your Customers and Clients Better**: You can do this by making sure you understand your customers' demographics and how you can expand them if you could. Can you reach more customers, or more affluent customers? If you change some of your services and products to cater to a new category of customers, what effect would that have on your business? Imagine having different tiers of services. There is always someone, or a group of someones, who want to be exclusive; can you offer them exclusivity, and at what premium? Obviously, you must always provide your best, and then some. Always aim to WOW them, and why not? This world is full of mediocre businesses. Now, imagine if you go out of your way and WOW your customers. This is obviously different for each business, and only you know how to do that. So many companies nowadays just try to get by; when they serve you, they go out of their way to make you feel they are doing you a favour, whereas it used to be the other way around.

You/your company doesn't need to move mountains for customers to WOW them; it could be the simplest things. I am sure anyone who has been to Japan and did some shopping perhaps noticed how they go out of their way to make you feel valued as a customer. It is an experience you will not forget. We are not talking about buying a Rolls-Royce, either; it could be a humble pair of cheap earrings or a souvenir.

Always find new channels for new customers while looking after the old ones. Make everyone feel valuable, old and new. Creating a strong 'caring for your customers' culture can only benefit the business.

6. **Market Yourself, Your Company and Your Mission**: In the previous section, we decided that one of the best marketing strategies is to start marketing your self-brand and make it an integral part of your business.

For a recovery marketing strategy, this can be done relatively easily and without costing the company a lot of money, namely by reaching out to existing customers and showing them that you are there for them if they need help. You can be as imaginative as you want to be and try to come up with new ways of getting the message across, but just a simple message saying 'We are here for you' can go a long way and revive some old dormant orders or need for your services, especially you incentivise them. Many years ago, I was just in the forecourt of a car dealership, browsing for a new car, when a car salesman approached me and presented himself as a new manager for the branch. He said if I was interested in a car, to let him know, and that he would do everything he could to make me happy; since he was new here, he wanted to sell as many cars as possible, and that meant he needed to be flexible. So far, over the past eight years, I have bought over six cars from him, for myself and other family members. Why? Because he was honest and didn't play tricks with me. Now, we are friends, and if I need anything car-related, he is my first choice. I thought I would mention this story because he told me the truth about the situation at the time. People know that, as business owners, now more than ever, we need customers, and what better way to say thank you for coming to us than by giving them an honest offer and being straight with them? People always appreciate honesty.

7. **Negotiate:** This is a good time to go back to your suppliers and possibly negotiate new terms of pricing, credit lines, delivery, etc.. The same goes for insurance and other business-essential connections. Everyone is in the same position, and the same way you try to help others and be unique by going out of your way, others will hopefully attempt to do the same. If they don't, then it is perhaps time to change that supplier or that insurance company.

Find good deals and strategically buy goods you need so that you don't run out of essentials that your business depends on without having more as a backup supply.

8. **New Experience:** This is a new experience for everyone, including you and your customers. Therefore, try to make the most of it by staying positive and coming up with ideas on how to be better at everything you do, which is potentially your ticket to thrive!

As the late Jim Rohn said, 'Never wish life were easier; wish that you were better,' He also believed that, 'What's simple to do is also simple not to do.'

Some of the ideas mentioned here are simple to do and may not be revolutionary, but the idea is to keep doing them repeatedly and for a long period of time in order for the magic to happen. You may concentrate on the immediate recovery plan and try to navigate the survival stage, which is what everyone is in at the moment. That is fine, but bear in mind that if you go back to business as usual, like before, it will only get you back to this point again, if you're are lucky! As we all know, most small businesses don't make it pass this point. As the economy is taking a downturn, and because you promised yourself that, no matter what, you will stay positive and do better than before, you need to make these changes part of your plan and start implementing them, but in a consistent fashion, adding more and more layers. For example, you can create a compound effect culture in your business, in that anything you do, sell or serve should have a multilayer service attached to it in order to serve even better. This way, you are giving your clients better service by allowing them to have everything under one roof, while the company also benefits in the long run. We are all familiar with the notions of upsell and downsell, and so on. Imagine creating another level of service on top of what you already have, making it a multi-tier service, or attaching a service to a product from your niche. How much more would that support your business in the future?

But, what about referrals? This is perhaps the second most direct way of increasing revenue and thriving by getting more customers, clients, members and guests. Small business owners know how important this is due to the word-of-mouth business they depend on, and yet, tragically, they do not peruse it actively. Some feel shy, and others avoid it out of fear of rejection; both are bad news if you want your business to thrive.

9. **Dominate Your Niche Market:** This is all about positioning. Being very good at whatever you are doing is probably what made you have a business today. You must have had a good idea or excelled one way or another in doing, serving or selling something to someone, which prompted you to set up a business. Now, what if you become the master of what you are doing and be the best? Going deeper and specialising in a particular niche may sound like leaving a lot of other work and money on the table that otherwise you could have

done, but the truth is, people pay much more for your service if you are the 'go-to person' in your market, and this is not difficult to achieve. First, you need to educate yourself on a deeper level about what you want to do, testing and testing to make sure everything is beyond expectations. Then, it is time to market yourself. There is nothing wrong with marketing yourself like crazy and charging a premium, if you can back it up with your delivery. While we are at it, why not have a guarantee system that beats everyone else? Stand out! It can only lead to a successful and thriving business.

You can already start this at the recovery stage by searching for what you like to do the most and how to do it, presenting yourself as the 'go-to person' in this economy, as long as you do it honestly and with other's interests in mind. People are happy to pay more as long as they get what they want.

10. **Grow to Thrive:** Now that you have followed the advice step by step, and you have made sure your infrastructure is supporting some form of normal function, you've ticked all the boxes, are doing marketing and branding yourself and, most importantly, you have a contingency plan for any future disaster, you are ready. There are many more aspects to running and making a business very successful, but there is only so much space in a book to cover all that.

However, we have learned a very valuable lesson during this pandemic, and that is, as the old saying goes: Don't put all your eggs in one basket.

I happen to know people who actually did very well during this hardship because their business model was selling online. Most of them were not affected; if anything, revenue for the likes of Amazon grew even further.

Do what you do best and look after your business, but, at the same time, diversify!

Try to have multiple income streams in the future. It doesn't matter how much that might be, but at least something will be generating revenue if another aspect of your business has stopped temporarily for whatever reason.

It will make you not so vulnerable in the future, because if your business is the only source of revenue, then you open yourself to the risk of being at the mercy of the next natural disaster, economic downturn, health crisis, fierce competition and so on. Most successful people have multiple streams of income. For example, a very successful online retailer once said that they are investing in brick-and-mortar business in case some aspect of online business shuts down completely. The same goes for a traditional brick-and-mortar business, who should have an online presence and other business presences in various niches. People always need to buy something, whatever that might be. Spend time on brainstorming and research, and see what is considered a good stream of income to add to your portfolio.

Have a portfolio of businesses, not just one that everything depends on.

THE LAST WORD | YOUR INVITATION

As we can see, we have covered many aspects of a successful business recovery plan. The key is proper goal setting and implementation. Even if we implement only a few ideas at a time, it is still better than doing nothing. Remember Jim Rohn's quote:

> *What's simple to do is also simple not to do.*

I hope this book can be used as a base for strategies that you can launch many successful endeavours from. Absorb the information, make it apply to you, follow the steps discussed earlier and watch how one small change can open the door for many more opportunities. Never forget to market yourself and your services.

For whatever reason, if you find yourself in a situation where you are not implementing these steps consistently to get the compound effect, or you're finding it overwhelming, or maybe you are just procrastinating, remember that you can change that, and we are here to help.

We have put together an entire system and programme just for this to be implemented in a successful way.

Most of us know what to do, but don't do it for one reason or another. We are here to help if you need us. We have programmes specifically tailored for the small-medium business, and if you have the desire to know more about these programmes, and how they could help you and drive you to success, then get in touch, and we will be happy to help you and get you to the top.

I have prepared a roadmap and a 'FAST Implementation' workbook to follow the important steps mentioned in this book in order to get into action FAST.

To get your copy of this workbook or for any consulting or coaching programmes that complement the book for a super-fast recovery plus many additional tools for your business,

please visit:

www.businessnotasusualbook.com

ABOUT THE AUTHOR

Dr. Diyari Abdah MBA MSc has had over thirty years' experience as a leader in his field, co-authored two bestselling books with Brian Tracy and Sir. Richard Branson. He is an Emmy Award-nominated producer for the humanitarian documentary—Armonia. He is also an international speaker and trainer. Dr. Abdah is an Adj. Assistant Professor at UIC Chicago (USA) and practicing in Cambridge (UK) where he also is the president of DA Academy for international speakers and trainers. His passion for helping others achieve their goals in life and business has been well received by many all over the world through training and coaching individuals and businesses. For further information visit www.businessnotasusualbook.com.